MARKETING WITHOUT MONEY for Small Businesses!

246 FREE and cheap ways to increase your sales!

Nicholas E. Bade

HALLE HOUSE PUBLISHING
5966 Halle Farm Drive • Willoughby, Ohio 44094–3076

More Marketing Without Money for Small Businesses!
246 FREE and cheap ways
to increase your sales!

First edition, first printing

Bulk discounts and workshops

Quantity discounts are available for educational and sales promotion use. For information, call (216) 585–8687. Or write to the publisher at the above address. See back of book for details about marketing workshops for your organization.

Disclaimer

This book has been researched and written with great care to provide accurate and useful information. But we cannot be responsible for any consequences resulting from the use of these tips. Additionally, this book is sold with the understanding that no one involved with it renders legal or other professional services. If you need expert assistance, seek the services of the appropriate professional person. Also check local laws and exercise good judgment.

Trademarks

Trademarked names are used throughout this book. Rather than put a trademark symbol in every occurrence of a trademarked name, we state that we are using the names only in an editorial manner and to the benefit of the trademark owner with no intention to infringe on the trademark.

Publisher's Cataloging–in–Publication

(Prepared by Quality Books Inc.)

Bade, Nicholas E.

More marketing without money for small businesses! 246 FREE and cheap ways to increase your sales! / Nicholas E. Bade.

p. cm.
Includes index.
Preassigned LCCN: 94–079474
ISBN 1–882923–15–4

1. Marketing--Cost Control. 2. Small business--Management. I. Title.

HF5415.122.B32 1994 658.8

QBI94–2286

Proudly printed in the United States of America.

Contents

1

Four essential steps for budget sales success

Small businesses all over America have successfully used the tips and techniques in this book to increase their sales.

But small businesses that successfully promote on a limited budget also do something else. They first apply four basic marketing principles. And whether you're just starting out or have a long established business, these principles could determine the success or failure of your promotional activities.

Observe the following principles and you will greatly improve your prospects for success!

1. Find a unique market niche or position

Position or positioning is making your goods and services stand out from the crowd. It's giving people a concrete reason to do business with you. Ask yourself:

Why would anyone in their right mind do business with you?

What do you offer potential customers that they can't get someplace else? What do you do better than anyone else?

The challenge is to create a positive distinction or difference between you and your competition. You can do it in many ways. You can tailor your products and services to the exact needs of a particular market group or geographic area. Or your distinction can be price, quality, service, reliability, variety, expertise, hours, or a combination. Whatever it is, your distinction is your market niche or position.

If you can't see a tangible positive distinction, you must create one. Otherwise, people have no reason to deal with you. But having a unique market niche is just a start. You must also translate your uniqueness into a benefit potential customers can easily understand and appreciate. So the second step is:

2. Identify your BIG customer benefit

When potential customers first consider your product or service, they ask themselves "What's in it for me?"

The answer to that question is your **BIG benefit**. Too many businesses talk about the features of what they sell. But a feature only describes what something is. Avoid that common mistake by selling benefits because a benefit explains what something does—how it solves a problem for the buyer or fulfills some need or desire. Benefits are what prospects buy.

To pinpoint your BIG benefit, look at what you offer from the prospect's perspective. See what your goods and services do for them. If you're not sure, talk to your customers. Ask why they use your product or service. The answers may surprise you since two people often see the same thing in opposite ways. Another thing that may surprise you is how little you know about your customers. That's why the third step is:

3. Pinpoint your prime prospects

The object is to find the fewest people who can do you the most good. And the more you know about them, the better you can target your scarce time and money.

In many instances, what you sell or your location will determine who they are. But most of the time, you'll need to identify who could benefit most from what you are selling, where they are and how to reach them. The best way to do this is to build a profile of your prime potential customers.

Your profile should include descriptive variables such as sex, age, address, occupation, income and education to name just a few. You may want to add variables that describe behavior or ways of thinking. Examples are media preferences or the types of vehicles they drive.

Additional valuable information is available—free—through the market research techniques and sources described in this book. Before you do any research, draw up a list of things you need to know. Keep it short, under a dozen questions.

Once you've identified your prime prospects, you'll know exactly who to target for the best sales results. Now, put it all together by preparing a brief written plan.

4. Prepare a brief written plan

You may prefer to wing it like so many other entrepreneurs and small business people. Don't! Businesses with a formal plan are more likely to succeed than those without one. Even a one or two page plan covering a full year will suffice—if you take the time to *write* it down.

Why write it down? Writing forces you to gather information, organize your thoughts, make decisions. A written plan states where you want to go and how you expect to get there. It is also a constant benchmark for checking your progress.

But more than anything, a written plan is a personal commitment. It is a statement of results for which you are willing to hold yourself accountable. Here's what to include:

Start with a situation review. In it, briefly assess your current situation. Describe your market niche, evaluate competitors, profile your customers. Explain what you think will happen in the upcoming year and how you will deal with it.

Next, set goals. Decide what you want to accomplish. Aim high but be realistic. Make your goals specific, measurable.

After that, plan your moves! Describe the exact steps you will take to reach your goals. Include due dates so you can track your progress or lack thereof.

Finally, draw up a budget. Decide what you will spend, when, where, why and how. Above all, try to forecast how much revenue—and profit—each expenditure will produce.

Unfortunately, no matter how hard you try, your plan will fail—if you base it on guesswork and opinion. You need cold hard facts. And the best way to get them is through market research. That's why this book includes plenty of free and cheap do–it–yourself research techniques.

Make something happen—NOW!

A written plan obviously does not guarantee success. But at least you will know where you are going—and when you get there. At the same time, don't get tied down or carried away with planning. It's important since planning helps you avoid basic mistakes that cause many small businesses to fail.

But the bottom line is: Nothing good happens in business until you sell something—you have to make something happen! And the rest of this book will help you do just that! So roll up your sleeves and start doing something concrete to boost your sales and profits NOW!

2

Cheap and easy ways to boost sales

Start with a name that sells!

Most small business owners fail to cash in on the single biggest form of FREE promotion available to them—the name they give their businesses.

The name you give your business is critical because it is the first—and perhaps the only—thing most potential customers will ever know about your business. Your name will largely determine their first impression of you. It is also the one thing that is seen and heard the most. Simply put, the right name is a powerful—and ongoing—source of FREE promotion! Yet few names are picked with consideration for sales implications. The key is to give your business a name that sells!

A name that sells does two things. First, it tells your target prospects exactly *what* you do. And, second, it tells them *why* they should do business with you. The *why* is your big benefit! Consider the name Budget Rent–A–Car. Is there any doubt what they do and why you should do business with them?

Think before you pick a name. Forget trendy, short–lived names with double meanings, negative connotations. Ignore names that are confusing, hard to find in the telephone book, difficult to spell, understand and remember. Organizations planning to enter new fields should look for a name that will cover future endeavors.

Family names are an easy way to avoid possible legal costs. But they give up a lot unless you are well known. Kenny Rogers, for instance, gave instant recognition and credibility to the restaurant chain named after him.

Established companies with a poor name may have to live with it. But if you are just beginning or are relatively new, unload the albatross. The long–term benefits will outweigh any initial grief. What's in a name? Big bucks—if it reaches and sells your prime sales prospects.

Business card: Your top sales weapon!

Millions of business cards change hands every day. But few actually sell! Look at yours . . . right now! Do you see a sales stimulating ad that makes the reader want to buy what you are selling? Does it even tell the reader what business you're in? Or is yours a plain, barely readable piece of cardboard?

A good business card should be your number one budget sales weapon because it's cheap—yet has a million uses. You can also say anything you want and use color, artwork or other attention getting features. You can even print several versions. So if you deal with priests one day and promoters the next, you can tailor your card accordingly.

Whatever you do, print tons of cards. Carry a big supply and give them to anyone who can even remotely help you. And leave them any place where they might do you some good.

How to make your card sell

When you prepare your business card, cover the basics. Include your company name, your personal name, address, area code, voice and fax numbers. Think twice about odd shapes, sizes and vertical layouts since they don't fit standard filing formats. Above all, make sure what you do leaps off your card! Finally, make your card readable. Use easy to read ink colors and 10 point or larger type. It sounds trivial but is quite serious since millions of people can't read the small type on many business cards. Why chance losing a sale because a prospect couldn't read your card?

Door to door delivers!

Delivering sales material door to door is a budget marketer's dream. Out of the hundreds of bargain basement techniques available to you, this could be one of the best because:

1. You can target prospects with hard–to–beat accuracy. Zero in based on geography, neighborhood demographics, type of residence, price range and other basic criteria.

2. It's cheap. The only out–of–pocket expenses are preparation, printing and distribution.

3. Instant results. You can use time–sensitive coupons and other gimmicks to generate quick results.

4. You get exclusivity. Door to door is no longer widely used. Your valuable message may be the only sales material at the prospect's door that day. It almost certainly will be seen—and read. Contrast this to direct mail where your piece might go totally unseen in a flood of mail.

5. Finally, there's delivery format flexibility. You can use plastic bags or flyers that hang on door knobs. But cutting the hole in the bag or flyer requires die cutting which can be very expensive. To save money, buy precut forms at a paper supply store or from a printer. You can also rubber band your piece to the knob, wedge it in the frame or stick it under the door.

As for distribution, you can use a professional service. A low–cost alternative is to hire students or cut a trade with local

Scouts or another community organization. **Warning!** It's illegal to put nonpostal material in mail boxes. Also check local ordinances covering door–to–door soliciting.

Classified ads have big advantage

Classified ads enjoy an enormous advantage over most other promotional vehicles—potential customers voluntarily seek out and read them. That means the reader almost always is in the mood to buy. And there's more good news.

Classifieds are versatile. There is a publication and listing category for every budget. Classifieds also cost nothing to produce and are easy to write and change. Classifieds have sold virtually everything.

Right placement critical. Classified success depends on running yours in the right place. So experiment. Try different publications and listing categories. Start with obvious headings, but investigate related or even distant categories. Go beyond your daily newspaper. Check neighborhood, African-American, ethnic, foreign language, religious and specialty newspapers or magazines.

Test with classifieds. Try different publications and listing combinations. Monitor results. Classifieds are also a cheap way to test new ad themes for expensive display ads. Simply prepare classifieds with ad messages you are considering. Then rotate them regularly in a single publication and compare results.

Grab your prospect's attention. Most people don't read past the headline so make yours leap off the page. Display it in bold type and capital letters. Incorporate your most powerful benefit in your headline. And use the persuasive sales words described elsewhere in this book.

Write to sell. Write as if you were speaking to just one person.

Stick to selling only one idea in each ad. Include enough facts for your prospect to reach a buying decision—and ask for the sale. For example, close with a phrase like "call now for $5.00 catalog." Provide telephone number and credit card information to complete a sale. Avoid confusing abbreviations and jargon. Spend a little more to get the job done right.

What you will pay. Actual rates are based on the number of words, lines or inches in your ad. Many publications offer extended contract rates that can reduce your per–insertion cost. But beware. Make sure you can change your ad periodically since an ad that runs repeatedly loses some impact. Develop several ad versions and rotate weekly to stay fresh.

50 FREE places where flyers reach prospects!

Pennies. That's all it costs you to reach prime prospects with flyers and signs—if you know where to put them. Listed below are 50 places where you should distribute flyers and post signs to increase sales:

Your own business. Out front. On nearby streets and corners. At transit and subway station entrances or stops. At other offices, stores, places in your development, mall or building. Under windshield wipers. And at establishments where you have arranged cross promotion deals.

Apartment building magazines bins. Apartment and condominium complex party centers. Utility poles. Counters and display racks at public places. At ethnic, social, religious, fraternal clubs. At club meetings. Church functions, synagogue activities, school happenings. Public sporting events. Concerts. Political rallies. Military cafeterias, PX's, recreation centers. Laundromats. Supermarkets and drugstores.

Through door–to–door distribution. In your mailings or those by others. Hand outs at trade or association shows. At expositions, flea markets, street fairs, mall fairs, outdoor and home shows. As a stuffer in your bags or in other establishments' bags. Newspaper or magazine insert.

In Welcome Wagon kits, community information packets, realtor information kits for newcomers. Libraries. Chambers of commerce. Tourist information centers and booths.

Hotel and motel racks, counters. Car service center and tire store waiting rooms. Medical and other professional offices. Senior recreational facilities and service centers. Give to friends, relatives, customers to distribute to their friends and neighbors. Bowling alleys. Roller and skating rinks. Depending on how picky you are, that's actually 55 locations. All offer a unique bonanza if you are persistent enough to get your sales material posted or distributed.

How to cash in on bulletin boards

Of the 50 or so places for flyers, public bulletin boards may be the best. They can reach large numbers of people for next to nothing. You can also pinpoint specific target markets by selecting the right boards and using a customized message.

Boards are commonly found in public facilities, supermarket and drugstore entrance ways. But don't overlook colleges, libraries, churches, hospitals, factories, banks, union halls, convenience stores and shopping malls as well as the many fraternal, ethnic and social clubs.

Boards are a low–cost source of sales leads for home–based businesses such as typing services, handcrafters and trades people. They also work well for lawn care, auto repair, home improvement and other widely needed basic services. Additionally, boards are ideal for people who provide personal care services and products.

Your posting can be a simple flyer or, better yet, the biggest sign allowed. If you have resources, create large, bold posters tailored to the location. Always include along the bottom tear–off tabs with your name, address and telephone number or take–one cards. To create a low–cost take–one card holder, fold up the bottom third of your sign and staple it to form a pocket. If the bulletin board owner wants a posting fee, barter your wares or services.

Hand out flyers in public places

Don't dismiss handing out flyers on street corners and other public places. It's frequently done with great success. Advantages include extremely low cost and the ability to target highly select audiences. A luncheonette, for example, can give out flyers at lunch time to everyone leaving area office buildings. You can also target recipients by sex, age, race, type of clothing worn and anything else you see. A men's wear store can hand out flyers to only well–dressed men, those wearing youth–oriented clothing, etc. Where it suits your purpose, include coupons and other inducements.

Windshield wiper flyers clean up!

Sticking flyers under car windshield wipers is a solid way to build business. To begin with, it's inexpensive. Printing and distribution time are your only costs. You also have the prospect's full attention since your ad doesn't have to compete with other ads. Best of all, it's easy to target a specific market.

You can distribute flyers on the basis of a vehicle's price, model, age, style, where it is parked, date, time and anything else you can think of. A health club, for example, might place flyers on cars that appearance–conscious people tend to drive. A body shop might target vehicles that need body work. Similarly, an auto detailer might focus on luxury and sports cars. As always, tailor your sales piece to the market.

Some situations may demand a tasteful business card ad, others a bold, bright flyer. Needless to say, exercise good judgment. Be careful when and where you place flyers. Exercise common sense. If you are challenged or told to stop, politely apologize and leave promptly.

Insert sales material in unusual places

Two businesses handing out each others coupons is a common cross promotion. But why stop there? Insert promotional material in each other's products. A bookstore might insert someone else's flyer in every book sold. A luggage store can get travel agents to stick information in airline ticket envelopes. A local coffee distributor or dairy might ask an egg supplier to put coupons in egg cartons.

The idea is to find a channel no one else is using to reach a lucrative target market at low cost.

Provide after hours take–one box

Set up a box or rack outside your establishment with information packets prospects can take when you're closed or not there. Many realtors, retailers and professional service providers report good success with this approach. It works especially well if you are located in a mall or someplace else that has walk by traffic. Also consider exchanging take–one racks and displays with compatible businesses. Don't forget to encourage passers by to take your material by adding the words "free—take one" to your display.

Ad specialties: How to use them right

Ad specialties are free gifts—those lovable little toys, trinkets and things businesses give out to create goodwill, generate sales leads, build name recognition and, hopefully, sales.

They are cousins to premiums which are gifts you receive for buying another product or service.

Most ad specialties are imprinted with the giver's name, address, telephone number and a sales slogan. Here's how to make these goodies sell for you:

1. Use to create name awareness and recall. Numerous studies show they can help keep your name in front of potential and current customers.

2. Don't use them alone. Ad specialties work best when supplementing other marketing efforts.

3. Keep copy short. We're talking about pens, matchbooks and other small space articles. Your message must be brief.

4. Plan ahead. Production times can range from three to eight weeks or even longer. Plan months ahead—this is especially important to get the lowest prices. Try to pool your purchases with friends, other businesses. See what your trade associations and industry groups offer.

6. Watch 'em! Ad specialties have a way of disappearing that's directly proportional to the size of your company. If you don't lock them up securely, your novelties will vanish into the homes, hands and pockets of everyone—except your intended recipients.

7. Which are best? Ad calendars and pens are old standbys because everyone needs them. But try to find something that ties into your business. This is also one area where cleverness counts. Visit your local ad specialty house and look over the 15,000 different ad specialties that are available.

8. Pick your ad specialties carefully. You might find you need some ad specialties for a special application such as a trade show or sales calls. If you have a clear need for them, definitely buy yourself a supply. But consider your ad specialties carefully. Look for items you can use in a variety of ways and for years—not just once.

Balloons, blimps big and small

Look no further for some thrifty tricks to get your establishment noticed. Balloons and blimps will do it. Maybe you can't afford the Goodyear Blimp with your ad on its side. But there are plenty of other blimps and balloons of all sizes.

Consider really BIG balloons, the kind you tether to your roof or parking lot. A huge inflatable puppy hovering over a new pet shop will pull a crowd—and sales—fast. Smaller balloons are ideal giveaways, great for calling attention to special products in your store and perfect for contests—just stick gift certificates in certain balloons.

Try ad specialty stores for small balloons in all shapes and sizes. They will even paint your name and logo on it. Before you rent, contact suppliers. Beer companies, for example, often furnish inflatable beer cans, mascots and other attention getters. They are ideal for street fairs, grand openings and other events.

Cash register tape ads and coupons

Small ads or coupons printed on the back of store cash register tape receipts are now available throughout much of the country. Businesses that most commonly offer this advertising medium include drugstores, supermarkets and other busy retail establishments. The medium's key advantage is your ability to hit a specific audience.

The cost per person reached won't be cheaper than many alternatives. But you won't waste money selling to numerous nonprospects since you will be targeting a precise market. If you feel this medium can help you, simply contact the establishment you have in mind. As always, offer to trade or barter. If you have a retail business, offer to trade tape space with appropriate noncompetitive establishments. Remember to promote your own business on the back of your tapes.

Community and school calendars

Community and school calendars are a low–cost way to build name awareness and goodwill in specific communities and school markets. To advertise, contact local schools. As for community calendars, you should find the producer's name right on the document. If you can't find a calendar for the area or school you want to hit, call School Calendar Company, Inc. at (800) 251–0970. This firm produces calendars for 4,000 high schools, colleges and communities nationwide.

School publications

While checking out calendars also look into school yearbooks and programs since they are useful for targeting students and their parents. Ads are generally inexpensive and you may be able to barter or trade for space. If you depend on student traffic or sell to their parents, consider school publications. Include a coupon or sales incentive in your ad to track results.

Decals, stickers remind

Stickers and decals can reinforce other efforts to promote new products or keep your name in the public eye at low cost. Credit card decals on store doors are a perfect example. If you sell through other businesses, you may want to furnish your own "Jones Parts Sold Here!" decals.

Colorful stickers with a brief sales message are great for promoting a new product or service. Just slap one on every envelope, package or whatever that leaves your place. You can also stick them on outdated brochures you can't afford to reprint. Print a sticker that reads "Overnight repair service now available—call for details!"

Especially useful is a bright sticker with your company name, address and telephone number. Stick several on every box you ship so anyone who handles the carton will know how to reach you, especially for reorders.

Church bulletins—prayerful promotion!

Sharp local merchants have advertised in church bulletins for years to reach a highly defined market at a low price. This is especially true of stores, services and trades people who depend on neighborhood patronage. Church bulletins vary like everything else.

Some are well read while others are promptly discarded. Some even have professional media representatives. Therefore, get the usual circulation figures, congregation demographics and other basics. Also keep in mind that many churches now have substantial drive–in congregations—so you may not get effective neighborhood coverage if that's what you want. Additionally, try not to pay cash for your ad. Trade goods, services or time.

Matchbooks trite but time tested

Matchbooks aren't a marketing miracle. Then again, they aren't bad for reaching smokers and other people who use matches frequently. Matches can help keep your name and a short sales message in front of potential customers. You can also include a coupon or information that requires the reader to take follow–up action. You then put respondents on your mailing list. And that's another plus.

You can give out matches at your business or distribute them through cigarette machines. Start by calling match producers who can brief you on design tips, costs and distribution options. Press hard for distribution details since that's the key to matchbook marketing. If you proceed, try a short test with a coupon or something that induces the matchbook user to call or send for more information.

Restaurant place mats sneaky

Look into restaurant place mats because they let you pinpoint prospects—and sneak into their heads by being there when most people have nothing else to occupy them. They are also ideal for cross promotions.

If you run a restaurant, promote your own specials and banquet space. Or sell the space to other merchants. Similarly, businesses should offer to buy place mats for a restaurant in trade for ad rights. You can tailor mats to specific restaurants, clientele, even time of day. For instance, breakfast mats might target seniors while lunch mats aim at business people. Add coupons, other tear–off devices to measure results.

Consider movie screen advertising

Movie screen ads are a good way to reach a highly defined market segment at a reasonable cost. The reason is most movies are targeted to specific audiences. If an upcoming movie will draw your target market, you should check into ad rates. Movie screen ads are also ideal for businesses such as restaurants, miniature golf courses and other places patrons might go after a movie.

Consider a tie–in promotion. A restaurant, for example, can cash in by offering a free beverage or discount when presenting a current day's ticket stub. Call local theaters for details and availability.

Trade for movie screen publicity

You may have a parking lot that's empty at night or weekends while a nearby theater or other business needs more space. Let them use your lot in trade for an on–screen ad at the show or other promotional considerations. Also look for products and services you can trade for screen spots.

Pissoir promotions—and more!

Sometimes you can reach target prospects at the strangest times and places. Advertising panels over men's restroom urinals are a good example. These are available in men's rooms at many restaurants, dance clubs and bars, especially those catering to young singles. Many ladies' restrooms also have ad panels in various conspicuous places. Then there's the possibility of ads on stall doors and hand dryers.

Look like a helpful friend

Instead of a formal sales letter or brochure, send prospects a photocopy of your sales letter. But first attach one of those yellow Post–It notes with a personal handwritten message. Say something like, "Fred, I thought you might find the attached information useful! Best regards, Bob."

You can use a common name or your own. Either way, your sales piece will look like it came from a caring friend or associate. People who have tried this approach swear by it.

Squeeze sales from inside mail

Always stuff coupons, flyers, ad reprints and other sales material with invoices, statements, bill payments and all outgoing mail. Promote new products, services, a sale, sneak previews and any other reason why your customer should buy something else from you. Where appropriate, include discount coupons aimed at the person who is likely to open the mail, rather than the actual addressee. If you send out statements, always include an order form that customers can return with their payments—it's a proven way to increase sales from current customers.

Make stationery, boxes sell

Make your stationery earn its keep by having a brief sales slogan or message printed on all your stationery and envelopes. Also print up a bright sales sticker. Slap several on every outbound box and carton. Include your company name, address and phone number so anyone who handles the box can easily reach you for reorders. Additionally, most postage metering machines let you add a sales slogan next to the postage. If yours has this feature, take advantage of it.

Post cards keep you in touch

Post cards are a fast and frugal way to keep in touch with your customers on a regular basis.

You can announce new products, private sales, special events, distribute coupons or say thank you. They also save you money. For starters, you don't need an envelope. Post cards are inexpensive to print and cost a third less than a letter to mail. Another bonus is extra exposure since everyone who handles the card sees your message. Furthermore, you reach people who don't always open advertising mail.

To cash in, use a big, bold catchy headline. Keep remaining copy short. "Bullet" your copy so it's readable at a glance. Print extra cards and hand them out at your business and other places. And while you're chasing new sales, show appreciation for current customers. Prepare a thank you post card and keep a stamped supply on hand for immediate use whenever a sales transaction exceeds a certain amount.

Send birthday, purchase anniversary cards

Most people only receive birthday cards from their spouses and immediate family. Try to remember your key clients on their birthdays. Instead of expensive cards, use a handwritten personal note. Additionally, send birthday cards on the anniversary of a big sale such as a house, car or major appliance—especially if the item is nearing the end of its useful life.

Sell through 'thank you' notes

Send a thank you note every time you get good service or someone does something for you. Include your business card and write on it "I enjoyed your great service—I hope you will try mine so I can reciprocate!"

We all love recognition and praise. When we get it, we're happy—and in a positive frame of mind for what comes next. In this case, your commercial.

3

Personal sales, referral and networking tips

How top sales people sell

Successful sales people always observe three P's: Prepare, practice, personality. Prepare by learning all you can about a potential customer's needs and wants. Then bone up on your product or service.

Next practice on a friend or associate. Find weaknesses in your pitch. Resolve problems. Address possible objections. Now, go sell—with personality. That comes from listening carefully to your customers. It sounds easy but most people cannot listen well. They are usually thinking about what they will say next — that's when you miss important sales clues from your prospect. Discipline yourself to listen and learn.

Remember to ask for the order

Don't laugh. An incredible number of sales people from minimum–wage store clerks to hot–shot veterans fail to ask for the sale in a clear, unmistakable manner. This generally happens when the potential customer seems disinterested or turned off. Ask anyway since the prospect can only say no. Train all your employees to do the same. Review all your sales material and forms.

Many sales pieces fail to include basic lines like "order now—call today" or "supply limited—call today and stock up now!"

Don't just tell—sell!

You meet scores of new people—and potential customers—every day. While shopping, running errands, at the gym, everywhere. Give them all a sales pitch. Sometimes you have to sell softly, especially at social events. Even so, always get in your commercial.

How? Prepare and rehearse a brief but thorough sales pitch. Keep it under 25 words. Use plain, simple language. Tell listeners exactly what you do—and how it will benefit them or someone they know. For example, a marketer might say, "I help businesses increase their sales and profits through affordable marketing and promotional programs."

30 sources for referrals

Chances are you have referral sources under your own roof—and all around you! Start with everyone you know. Here's some imagination joggers: Present and former co–workers. Neighbors of all ages. People who serve you such as dry cleaner, food store, auto services, domestic help, baby sitter, hairdresser, barber, bartenders and waiters. Religious contacts like your minister or rabbi, congregation members.

And how about these: Professional relationships and services including your doctor, dentist, optometrist, psychologist, lawyer, accountant, financial adviser, realtor, insurance agent. Organizations such as Kiwanis, Knights of Columbus, Moose, Elk and professional societies. School contacts including teachers, administrators, other parents and PTA members, alumni, former classmates.

Need more? Try sports contacts like teammates, bowling

clubs, competitors, partners, people who frequent your health club. And, of course, your own family, relatives, their friends and acquaintances. The point is everyone is either a potential customer or can lead to one. A favorite bartender or host, for example, might be willing to give your business cards to target customers. A hairdresser or barber can talk you up to scores of prospects!

Sell at dinners, meetings

Chances are you spend countless hours at professional dinners, lunches and meetings or obligatory church, fraternal and social gatherings. In fact, you may attend these functions to develop sales—but only have fat to show for your time. To get the most from these efforts, start with a specific sales strategy. Step one is to remember you are there to work. Forget about eating or chatting with friends. Instead, prepare. Develop a tight one–minute sales pitch. Find out who's coming. Know in advance who you must see. Arrive early and meet everyone as they arrive. Exchange cards. Keep moving during the event and make all your key contacts. When the event ends, see everyone again as they leave. Finish by sending follow–up letters the same day to everyone you met. It's hard work but you'll trade calories for cash!

Be a joiner and network

Whether we like it or not, most people tend to buy from people they know. Depending on your business, you can capitalize by joining organizations, associations and clubs patronized by your prime prospects. Tread carefully because you can stretch yourself too thin and waste considerable time and money on organizations that do you little or no good.

Being a joiner probably won't yield fast results although it could. Nevertheless, you'll derive many benefits. You'll meet prospects, find partners for joint promotional activities, strengthen ties with current clients, keep abreast of your industry, contribute to your community or field—and make new friends while building your own business.

Do something to stand out!

Once you become a member of various organizations and clubs, you are likely to find many "joiners" like you. So you need to do something to stand out from the crowd. The hard way is to attend every meeting and to work on time–consuming committees and programs.

Unless you really like it, replace the work with ingenuity. Stage an attention–getting promotion that benefits members. Or contribute goods and services for door prizes at meetings and organization happenings. If you can, give each member a sample of your product or services, perhaps on their birthdays.

Join lead referral networks

Consider joining one of the clubs and networks that exist solely to exchange referrals and increase contacts. These "tips clubs" as they are often called give members a chance to explain their business to other members. Importantly, club members then commit to selling the other members to their clients and contacts. Members, in effect, become a sales force for each other. Members also purchase goods or services from other members.

Many clubs will only accept one member in a specific field or category to avoid conflicts and divided effort. As for cost, clubs usually levy a membership charge and an annual renewal fee. If you decide to join, be ready to work. After all, why should others hustle for you if you don't reciprocate? Check local business publications for clubs in your area. If there aren't any, start your own or launch a local chapter for a national network such as Pittsburgh–based Network Professionals, Inc. The number is 800–929–LEAD.

Solicit referrals from peers

Your clients and customers aren't the only source of referral business. You can also develop new sales and profits—free of charge—by asking peers and even competitors for business they can't handle. They may be overloaded or lack the expertise needed.

Contact your peers and competitors and ask for their overflow. Brief them on your credentials. If necessary, invite them to inspect your work and facilities so they are comfortable sending customers to you. Offer to reciprocate when you are busy. Finally, work out exactly how they refer work to you. Timing—and tact—are also critical. Above all, be trustworthy. You may wind up with someone's regular customer on a one–time basis due to some nonrecurring situation. Don't try to steal or solicit the customer. Word is likely to leak out and you'll hurt your future referral opportunities. Instead, work extra hard to make the referring party look good. That word will also get out and you'll benefit accordingly.

Promote through current projects

Anytime you are handling a project or job on–site, take time to make sales calls to nearby homes and businesses. At minimum, distribute sales material. If you provide a maintenance, improvement or installation service, invite neighbors over to see your work.

For professionals and services, handling a project for a client next door is often a great endorsement. For example, you can use your present project as an example of what you can do. Or you can use your current client's name to reach decision makers at nearby businesses. Better yet, try to get your current client to walk you over and introduce you.

Personally telephone or visit newcomers

Newcomers to your area could become customers for life—if you reach them before the competition does. Welcome Wagons are one way. But go a step further: Personally visit or call new residents in your service area.

New residents, especially those from out–of–town, may not have any friends or ties in the area and will appreciate the personal attention. You'll also catch them before they have a chance to look around for basic services. This approach is especially effective for dentists, doctors and other professionals. To get leads, watch real estate transaction columns in local newspapers. Additionally, set up referral deals with realtors, builders and suppliers. Also check into government records.

Make contacts through team sponsorships

Consider team sponsorships a subtle form of personal selling or networking, rather than promotion. Realistically, backing a local bowling team won't create instant sales. And 10 T-shirts with your name isn't exactly a massive publicity push.

But the right team will open opportunities galore to meet and cultivate current and prospective customers. You mix with them away from the office, distractions and competitors.

Call on 'SMERFES,' other groups

Group markets are a time–tested way to reach large numbers of prospects quickly and economically. If you need leads, start with the "SMERFES" groups—social, military, ethnic, religious, fraternal, educational and sports teams. Also go after these: Girl Scouts, Boy Scouts, churches, schools, Jaycees, senior centers and communities, civic groups. Or computer, photography, bridge, radio and other specialty clubs. Also area chambers of commerce, trade associations, restaurant and tavern owner associations, Rotarians, Kiwanis, Moose, Knights of Columbus, AA chapters, MADD, SADD, alumni and booster groups.

Apply personal touch to inactive accounts

Sometimes it only takes a little personal attention to resurrect dead or inactive accounts. Many accounts simply drift away because you haven't contacted them recently and they forgot about you. Still others stop patronizing you because of a real or imagined problem.

Spark new sales from inactive customers by contacting them and personally expressing your interest in their patronage. A short personal note letting them know you value their business might suffice. But to leave a real impression, take time to telephone or to make a face to face visit. Use the opportunity to probe. Find out if they are dissatisfied with something you've done or have found a better deal elsewhere. For added impact, offer them a reward or gift for giving you another opportunity to serve them.

Try tiny treats for tall sales edge

Expensive entertaining isn't the only way to win sales with food and drink. You can also capture hearts—and sales—with coffee, donuts and plenty of candy. This taste–bud tip works well on outside sales calls and at your business. Your simple hospitality humanizes an otherwise correct but impersonal transaction. You'll also reward and reinforce desired behavior. And if you treat every time, clients will look forward to your next get together.

Start simple. Buy inexpensive candy or barter with local candy distributors. Look for little individual portion bags. Include sugar–free candy for those who prefer it. **Spread your name** and goodwill around by giving treats to everyone you see on your sales visits, not just the person you meet.

Exploit seasons. Try candy eggs at Easter, chocolates at Valentine's Day. Use gimmicks. Don a costume occasionally. Around Halloween give out candy from a big orange jack–o'–lantern. Start a candy club. On your first visit, give away candy jars imprinted with your logo, name, address, telephone number and a simple sales message.

Refill the candy jars on your future visits. Serve coffee, donuts and other refreshments at your business. Encourage people to help themselves to your goodies—let them know you genuinely appreciate their patronage. Bring donuts on early morning sales calls. Most businesses have coffee but not the trimmings. Pass the box around and talk sales while your captive audience munches away.

Become an information pack rat!

The more you can personalize your sales efforts, the more likely you are to succeed. The answer? Become an information pack rat. Save every scrap of information you see or hear about potential clients. Look for things in common like colleges, clubs, hobbies, interests, military service and shared experiences. Then use your "data bank" in your sales activities. The obscure fact you gleaned from a local newspaper might be the perfect conversation starter.

4

How to get others to sell for you

Start your own word of mouth campaign!

Word of mouth *is* the most valuable way for a small business to survive and thrive. The reason is word of mouth is believable. Nothing, absolutely nothing, beats a personal recommendation. Unfortunately, word of mouth takes a long time to develop. But you can speed up the process by starting your own word of mouth campaign.

First, always ask your customers to tell others. It can be something as simple as a sign that reads: "Referrals gratefully accepted." Or ask for help. Say something like: "Thank you for the opportunity to serve you. We truly hope everything was outstanding. If you agree, please mention us to your friends. We survive only because customers like you tell your friends." It's trite but a simple, sincere request often works wonders.

You can also start your own word of mouth campaign. Call everyone you know—family, friends, associates, even acquaintances familiar or long unseen. Offer them a discount, a special, anything to try you. When they do, smother them with good service. Then ask them to go out and tell others. Also give them discount coupons to bestow on friends as a favor (see tips elsewhere).

Enlist help of key opinion molders

Depending on your business, let public figures and opinion molders sample your products or services. Give freebies to people who come in direct contact with your prime prospects—and ask them to pay you back by talking up your products and services. For example, a restaurant can give free meals and gift certificates to bellhops, motel desk clerks, chamber of commerce employees and others who are often asked for restaurant recommendations.

Similarly, providing free goods or services to local media personalities can pay off many times over. If you go this route, check first—many media people, especially news employees, are not allowed to accept freebies. In fact, many will be insulted regardless of their employer's gift policy.

Join forces with other businesses

Another cost effective way to reach new prospects for less is to team up with other businesses. Find noncompeting businesses that target the same customers as you. Natural tie–ins work best but aren't essential. Also try to find products or services that appeal to both customer bases.

Cooperative opportunities are plentiful. For starters, you can hand out each other's sales material. Stuff it in each other's mail. Send out a joint mailing. Trade window display space. Share a trade show booth. Or create sales packages in which you both offer special benefits. You end up with a deal that's doubly attractive to both partners' prospective customers.

You can also conduct joint sales incentive programs. One way is to offer incentives such as coupons and discounts to each other's customers. This value–added feature boosts your partner's sales—and yours. A restaurant might give a limousine company coupons worth $10 off dinner for two on a week night. The point is both businesses reach high potential prospects for a lot less than the cost of going it alone.

Become premium for other businesses

Most businesses only sell themselves directly to their ultimate customers. But you should work extra hard to package your wares as a premium for other businesses—you'll gain a lot while spending very little. Here's why:

1. Increased sales. You will create a huge new indirect market for your offerings. Businesses that use your products or services as a premium will also become new sales outlets and a new sales force for you.

2. Free publicity. Their promotional efforts will include your product, service or name. You'll receive valuable free exposure—perhaps more than you could generate on your own.

3. New customers. Everyone hates to waste freebies. People who wouldn't otherwise patronize your business may do so simply to use the premium. If they can't, they may give it to someone else. Odds are you'll win new customers either way.

4. Improved cash flow. You might get advance payment for many premiums that won't be used until a later time. Gift certificates are a good example. Realistically, most businesses will want to pay for the premiums as they are redeemed.

5. Free "breakage" money. Paid–for premiums are not always used or redeemed. People move. Or they lose, forget about certificates and the like. This gap or breakage is a dream because you have the income— without the corresponding expense.

To get on the premium bandwagon, explore natural tie–ins. A wedding dress shop, for example, might give out tanning salon gift certificates. But businesses don't have to be related. A restaurant certificate is something every business can use.

Sell through other businesses

You may be able to sell your goods or services to and through other businesses in your area. Let's say you operate a wallpapering business. Offer to provide papering demonstrations and classes at paint, wallpaper and do–it–yourself stores in trade for referrals and exposure.

Even if you have your own shop, you can still sell to others. Many bakeries, for example, sell goods to supermarkets and other stores. Also look for creative outlets for your product. A cookbook can be sold at restaurants, cooking equipment stores and gourmet food stores in addition to books shops. If you are just starting out, be willing to consign your goods. The idea is to find innovative new distribution channels and outlets to sell your offering.

Let defunct competitors sell for you!

Some of your competitors may be gone but not necessarily forgotten by former customers! Anytime a competitor stops operating, pick up the remains. Buy the old telephone number and install a new phone line. When people call it, advise them that So & So is out of business but that you can help them—offer a first time discount or premium. Also try to purchase the old company's mailing list and any other records. If they went bankrupt, hurry down to the local courthouse. Check for names of suppliers and others who filed claims. They could be good sales leads for you. Remember, a competitor may be gone but can still sell for you.

Turn customers into outside sales force

Give your regular customers the tools—and a reason —to sell your business. Offer them discount cards they can bestow as a favor on friends, family and associates. After all, everyone loves to be a big shot by handing out favors. You can also make it worth their while. Include a place where they can write in their names and address. Give them a gift whenever a specified number of cards is used. This technique also builds a mailing list of your best customers—so you can promote to them in the future.

Let employees give out VIP cards

Boost employee morale—and sales—by giving them VIP cards that entitle their friends and families to special discounts or services.

Include a line where the employee signs to validate the VIP card. This lets the recipient know the signer is special and boosts the employee's stature. As an added prestige factor, the discount can vary according to the employee's length of service and rank.

Don't let employees hand out cards at work. Have them do it elsewhere on their own time to help increase sales. To get even more mileage, conduct a sales contest based on card sales over a given period.

Reward employees for prospecting

Nonsales employees may not have sales skills but they have eyes—and can recognize a prospect when they see one. The trick is to motivate all your employees to constantly watch for sales prospects.

One way is to give them a financial reward every time they bring you the name of a genuine prospect. Work out rules in advance. If the prospect becomes an actual customer, reward the employee with another bonus. You can make it a percentage of the new customer's first order. Don't have a sales force? You do now!

Boost employee sales for 17 cents

You can increase the sales performance and work productivity of low–paid employees by praising them frequently. That's the finding of several research studies.

Most people don't work for money alone. They also want and need personal recognition—that's especially true of lower–level employees. In fact, many low–paying companies with aggressive human relations programs are among the country's most successful.

Praise is free yet most of us don't use it nearly enough. Solution? Resolve to give praise freely whenever your employees deserve it—get into the habit praising them immediately when warranted. Set a praise quota. Mark your calendar with a goal to give X number of compliments in a specified time period. Check your progress.

Above all, give tangible recognition. Supplement your verbal pats on the back with monthly gifts, plaques or simple certificates. For example, you can buy elegant blank certificates for around 17 cents each in quantities of 100. Simply customize them on any basic computer printer. To cash in, start a "sales star" or "employee" of the month club. Print your certificates, put them in frames and you have a great yet low–cost employee motivator.

5

Shows, exhibits and parties for the frugal

When to exhibit at shows

Trade shows, exhibits and other events deserve your attention because they are a proven way to meet large numbers of prime prospects—at far less cost than making individual sales calls. But there are thousands of shows ranging from trade shows to conventions, expositions, state fairs, county fairs, church bazaars, neighborhood festivals, chamber of commerce mixers and shopping mall fairs.

Which shows are best? The ones that will help you make the most money by letting you meet the largest number of potential customers for the lowest possible price. Bottom line? Show participation is justified only when (1) you are certain most attendees will be serious prospects and (2) you are determined to come home with sales or orders.

Skip shows when you aren't sure who will attend. Similarly, don't participate simply to display, demonstrate or educate people about your products and services. **Go to sell!** Focus everything on that goal and bring whatever you need to close sales—and take orders—on the spot.

You can also use shows to renew ties with former customers, strengthen current relationships, increase your visibility, build a "live" mailing list and gather hot sales leads for fast follow–up. Shows also help you monitor competitors and assess customer reaction to new products or services.

Whether these benefits justify the show cost depends on how important intangible benefits are to you.

Ten tips for successful show selling

The show exhibitor who freely hands out expensive brochures and waits to answer questions is wasting money. In reality, successful show selling is far more sophisticated and personally demanding. Here are ten tips to help you get more for your money no matter where you are exhibiting:

1. Resolve to talk to everyone. This will demand constant hard work and all the stamina and determination you can muster. But you must because studies show just *one* in 20 visitors is a hot prospect. You also need as many contacts as possible for follow–up calls.

2. Engage, qualify, eliminate. Aggressively engage everyone who comes by. Use warm, witty, neutral openers. Prepare specific questions that enable you to identify prospects who realistically can benefit from your offerings. Politely—but quickly—end conversations with nonprospects. Get information for future sales calls. Probe rapidly into prospects' needs.

3. Sell benefits at once. The average show conversation lasts under five minutes. Don't waste it. Immediately tell prospects how your product or service benefits them. Forget features. Focus on key benefits like cost savings and improved sales.

4. Appear inviting. Look like you want the visitor's company. Always stand because no one wants to disturb a resting person. And don't talk to friends or colleagues. After all, strangers are reluctant to interrupt a conversation. Above all, watch nonverbal messages. Keep your hands behind your back. It's comfortable and looks professional. Never fold your arms across your chest. This says "stay away from me!" Similarly, prospects assuming this stance may be skeptical, even hostile. Disarm them with neutral comments and warmth.

5. Don't oversell. If a prospect wants to write an order on the spot, go for it. Otherwise, state your benefits and arrange a follow–up meeting. Then let the visitor make her or his rounds while you engage prospects you might otherwise miss.

6. Plan carefully. Prepare a formal show plan. Study attendance, activity lists. Pick your best shots. Set specific contact and sales goals. Go in with a stated objective so you'll have a way to determine whether the show was worth it.

7. Sell ahead. Contact all prospects before the show. Send an invitation with your booth number and other particulars. Personally call key clients and best prospects. When the event begins, slip flyers under attendees' hotel room doors. Give them out at pre–exhibit parties, etc.

8. Staff for results. If you aggressively pursue everyone like you should, you will be physically exhausted and emotionally drained. Therefore, bring a team if you can. Limit shifts to three or four hours. Take frequent breaks away from the booth.

9. Train, rehearse. Prepare a tight, hardhitting sales presentation that fits the five minute time frame. Train everyone until they know it inside and out. Rehearse through role playing.

10. Control brochure expense. Keep in mind that 19 of 20 visitors are low level or nonprospects. Even so, most exhibitors lavish expensive brochures on everybody. Exercise fiscal common sense. Print a nice but low–cost flyer for mass distribution. Include information on how people can call or write you for your deluxe brochure. Save your high buck creation for prime prospects. Besides, most show handouts end up in file drawers and trash cans.

Sell prospects at free how–to seminars

You or your business may possess unique knowledge that others find interesting. Offer to conduct free seminars at schools, churches, condominium meeting centers and other organizations. How–to seminars for everything from buying insurance to hanging wallpaper would benefit the sponsoring organization—and give you a chance to sell serious prospects face–to–face. Additionally, you can ask for something in trade for your time.

Get a free ad or story in the group's publications, have them give out your sales literature or do anything else you can think of. If the seminar is open to the public, contact the media to receive free publicity through community events announcements and calendars.

Staging seminars on a shoestring

If you're providing the labor, the meeting room is potentially your main seminar expense. Before you rent, check out local community centers, schools and social clubs. Many will let you use a room free if you can show how your seminar benefits the community or their members. Most local hotels won't be this generous. But they might trade your goods or services for a meeting room. Or team up with a compatible business and run a seminar that offers broader coverage of a particular topic—you'll draw a larger audience this way while you share the expenses.

Free demonstrations persuade

Getting the prospect's attention is Job One in successful selling—and nothing beats a live demonstration where the audience can see, hear, smell, taste, touch or feel your wares. Add flair or a gimmick and your item will sell itself. How? Get your prospect actively involved with a free sample, a hands-on try, a challenge, an unusual display.

Conduct free demonstrations wherever your prospects gather or live. If necessary, run an ad promoting your appearance schedule. Above all, arm yourself with everything you need to complete sales on the spot. Bring helpers who can take orders—and money—while you sell.

Party your way to success

Home parties are the original form of networking and survive in our mass media era because they are cost–effective. You can target prospects. And, given an incentive, the party giver will sell for you—while participants usually feel obliged to buy something. Parties traditionally target women but resourceful marketers will also hold parties for men.

Hold customer appreciation parties

Throw a customer appreciation party periodically to strengthen current productive relationships, renew old acquaintances—and to ask for new business from closed or inactive customers. The happening offers you a positive excuse to call someone who is otherwise "unavailable" or unresponsive to you.

At the event, you can demonstrate or brief guests about new services and products. You can also make appointments for follow–up sales calls. As for the event, try for something unusual. Happenings can range from a simple cocktail party to an elaborate theme evening. Possibilities: A "We love your business!" Valentine Day party, Christmas in July, picnic at a local park, or a tie–in with the Super Bowl, a big boxing match or another popular sporting event. Strapped for funds? Co–sponsor an event with a compatible business or barter the party with your products and services.

'Subpoena' guests to your party

A gag subpoena that's actually your party invitation is guaranteed to get everyone's attention. Make your invitation look like a real subpoena. Then write legal but humorous copy such as "You are hereby ordered by the District Court of Good Times to appear at a party . . . ."

For even greater impact, dress up like a law officer and personally deliver your subpoenas. This approach has been used widely with excellent results.

6

Business basics that reap rewards

Train for gain

Employee training quickly yields increased sales. It's also a necessity since you are literally at the mercy of your staff. Still, most small businesses feel they can only afford to provide informal or sporadic on–the–job training. If that's you, here's a low–cost alternative.

Set aside 10 minutes daily for employee training. Initially, use the sessions to explain exactly what everyone's supposed to do—focus especially on how you want customers treated.

Next identify specific new things they can do to help boost your sales. Focus on those topics in subsequent training meetings. Results will improve because employees will know precisely what's expected from them—and they will be armed with new sales skills and strategies.

As you proceed, write everything down. It's a pain but soon you will have an employee manual—which will save you time and money training future hires. For instance, veteran employees can use the manual to train newcomers for you. You can also include policies and procedures in the manual that will help you avoid employment–related legal headaches.

Outconvenience competitors

Our nation is changing dramatically in terms of what businesses must do to accommodate potential customers. The problem is time—people have less than ever before. Two–income households are still increasing. People are working longer hours. Commuter distances are lengthening. More parents have to drop off, pick up children at day care.

For these people, time is precious. They are streamlining their lives to use time more efficiently. Out of sheer necessity, they are patronizing businesses that are easy to deal with. So make it easier for prospects to patronize you rather than competitors. Examine these basics from a prospect's viewpoint:

Hours, days of operation. Are you open or accessible when your prospects can conduct business? **Pay policies:** Do you accept all major credit cards, not just two? What about personal checks? Do you offer financing? **Telephone:** How fast are your phones answered? Do you offer 24–hour live service or fax, modem, machine, voice or E–mail service? What about an 800 number? **Convenience:** Do you provide pick up and delivery? After hours dropoff? **Accessibility:** Is your location well signed? Is your parking adequate? Do you provide clear location directions in sales literature?

Once you've reviewed these points, discuss them with your current customers. Sure, they are patronizing your business so you must be doing things right! Not necessarily. They may be accepting inconveniences that prospects won't tolerate.

Convenience is now widely recognized as a key factor in consumer buying decisions. Consequently, an ever increasing number of businesses and service providers are offering 24–hour service. Simply put, convenience means you are available and accessible when your prospects can or want to do business—not when it is traditional or convenient for you.

Clean for green!

You may be losing sales—right now—because your place of business looks sloppier than you realize. Read this section before you say "not me!" Then decide.

Right or wrong, prospects judge you, your goods and services by the appearance of your premises, vehicles, employees and business practices. First impressions are lasting. Appearance also is a quick way to gauge your competence or lack thereof. The proper "look" inspires confidence. Shortcomings trouble people and drive them away.

No one runs a crummy business intentionally—it creeps in unnoticed. Businesses start out clean, sharp. Then little things happen. One here, another there. You may not notice them because you are always there. But they add up—and turn off prospects who walk into your place cold. What can you do?

Exceed customer expectations

Turn grime into gold two ways. First, inspect your business monthly. Second, resolve to be the best in your field. Customers have a general idea how businesses like yours should look—so shoot to exceed the industry norm.

Common problems and remedies

1. Banish handwritten signs. No matter what they say, the real message is you cut corners. What's more, "temporary" signs often become permanent eyesores.

2. Zap tape and pins. A few pennies worth of yellowing tape can ruin expensive decorating. Remove old tape and pinned up signs. Anything worth posting should be framed and under glass to keep it clean.

3. Wash lights, fixtures. Film on bulbs and fixtures can make your place look dingy. Wash regularly. Don't forget to clean the inside of fixture cases.

4. Put away, remove clutter. You may lack storage space. So mail accumulates on desks, file cabinets. Boxes are piled in corners. Make space! Aggressively discard old stuff. Buy storage cabinets. Clear off desk tops every night—you'll start the next day with a fresh, upbeat new look!

5. Clean and repair. You would never let visitors to your home see worn, torn and frayed carpeting—or repairs with duct tape. Don't do it to valuable customers. Have professional repairs made at once. Also clean and fix desks, counters, chairs and furniture regularly. Inspect for damage every day.

6. Touch up nicks. Walls and doors endure an unavoidable pounding. Schedule regular touch ups. Whenever you have painting done, save extra paint for future needs.

7. Keep literature fresh. Too many businesses provide old, torn or inappropriate literature to waiting clients. Spring for current publications. Put out plenty of your sales brochures.

8. Control odors. Unpleasant odors can build up gradually so you don't notice them. But customers will. Religiously police trouble areas. Conversely, sell with positive smells. Try the aroma of fresh–brewing coffee, baking, flowers, popcorn, etc.

9. Please your worst critic. Find someone who is finicky and brutally frank. Ask this person to give you an honest evaluation of your establishment's appearance—from a customer's perspective.

10. Economical "new" look! When all is said and done, a good clean up and repair drive amounts to a low–cost remodeling—and provides a fresh new look you, your employees and customers will love!

7

Offbeat ways to grab attention and customers

Run for an office!

Win or lose, you can generate tons of free publicity and become well known in your community or organization by running for an office. In fact, many people run for office with no intention—or desire—to win. They just want the visibility. But you can also make numerous useful contacts. And running for office is a good way to influence the outcome of legislation or government actions that could hurt your business.

Whether running for president of your local chamber or a government position, follow the basic marketing principles in the front of this book. Know who you want to reach, what they want and how you fill that need. Develop well thought out positions on key issues and stick to them.

Write a book—it's easier than you think

Writing a book is a proven way to enhance your professional credentials, build credibility and create publicity. Yet it's easier and cheaper than you might think. Done properly, a book will pay for itself and produce a profit. You can even use it as a giveaway when you solicit business or in conjunction with seminars and other sales building activities.

The challenge is to find a topic that turns you on and will excite others. As for writing, you can find plenty of affordable editing help. Getting published is the real battle. Unless you have a really unusual subject, commercial publishers will probably turn you down.

An alternative is to publish it yourself. You can type set and produce a camera ready book on a home computer setup. Many professional book printers will provide 2,000 copies of a 100–page book for around $2,000. So for roughly $2.00 each, you have a one–of–a kind promotional item that sells you! **One caution:** Avoid those companies that offer to help you write and publish your book for a fee. Doing it yourself is usually cheaper and more productive.

Picket your own business!

Sign wielding pickets usually attract a crowd—and the media. So cash in by picketing your own establishment.

Hire friendly pickets. Equip them with colorful signs bearing messages like "Jones Furniture prices unfair to competition!" Or "Jones quality unfair to others!" And perhaps "Investigate Jones Furniture's low prices."

Try costumes and seasonal themes. Or tie your picketing to a sale, new product introduction or other notable event worth publicizing. Imagine a sidewalk full of bunnies promoting an Easter sale carrying signs that read "Hop in for town's lowest prices!" And "Ear's the place for best buys." Or "Now—eggstra low prices."

Before an election, consider "Jones Store—the working person's choice." And "Vote for Jones low prices." Christmas? How about "Jones low prices unfair to Santa!" Find someone who can write humorous or witty signs, post your pickets and call the media. It makes a great human interest story. You could receive thousands of dollars worth of free publicity—while boosting your sales.

Exploit competitor's big event

Don't let a rival's big event overshadow you. Instead, ride your competitor's coattails. If it's a grand opening, counter with an open house. Make your event sound like a grand opening so your competitor's customers mistakenly come to you. Place open house ads promoting various specials. Use a searchlight. Bring in a celebrity. Offer a ridiculously low "open house today" premium—but fight back.

Searchlights add urgency

Searchlights are a tried and true attention getter with a twist—they also create a sense of urgency. Most people know searchlights mean something is happening now so they are ideal for generating quick results.

Searchlights are excellent for grand openings or calling attention to a location. They are also well suited to night time events such as midnight sales and other late night happenings.

They are limited in how far away they will be seen. And, realistically, not too many people will drive out of their way to find the source of a searchlight. So they shouldn't constitute your total marketing effort.

Sky's the limit for selling!

Skywriters and airplane–towed banners can be seen by large crowds. Thus, they are frequently used at beaches, outdoor concerts and sporting events. They work best in combination with other promotional tools. But skywriting or airplane banners can be great alone if you have the right product or a clever idea. Several years ago, the New York Yankees were playing a big series in Boston. Trailways Bus Co. capitalized with a skywriting message that read "Yankees go home for $10 on Trailways!" If you believe your upcoming idea is novel, contact the media.

Silly stuff is fun for sales!

Silly promotions are a cheap way to show customers a good time, create publicity—and boost sales. Just do something really off the wall. An engineering firm, for example, might give safari suits to clients visiting a project in a rural area. And a restaurant might have a Silly Shirt Sunday or a Hawaiian Shirt Monday.

Anyone wearing proper attire gets free dessert, a 10% discount or other bonus. Or you might have a Halloween costume party in your store the end of every month. If you develop something really different, contact local media, especially if it offers a picture opportunity.

Random rewards spark sales

Create word–of–mouth advertising and sales by randomly rewarding good customers with surprise gifts. A restaurant, for example, might give randomly selected regulars a VIP certificate good for a reduced rate or complimentary meal on a slow night. Or when they go to pay the check, give them a surprise on–the–spot discount. The excited patron is bound to tell others what happened—especially if you ask them to do so. The customer may also bring friends along on the next visit or come in more frequently. Give out awards quarterly or every other month to control costs.

8

Signs and mobile ads spark sales

Billboards: Sales force that never sleeps!

Billboards are usually beyond the budget of most small businesses. Nevertheless, they might work for you in special circumstances. For example, there might be one strategically located billboard you can use to direct traffic to your door. Here's some pointers for billboards and outdoors signs of all sizes and types:

1. Billboards have strong impact because of their larger than life size. It's hard to miss or ignore a well–placed board.

2. They can reach your prospects at key times. Consider the impact of a directional billboard at a major highway exit.

3. Outdoor never rests. Outdoor signs sell 24 hours a day, seven days a week, year round. People see them over and over.

4. Be clear, concise. Most boards are aimed at auto traffic—and research shows the typical driver sees a billboard for five seconds or less. So a strong visual is desirable to convey your message. Also keep words to six or less—research indicates anything longer is unreadable! Use big, bold, clear type. Catch the eye with strong color and a great graphic.

5. Results are slow. Outdoor normally does not produce fast sales unless it reads "Last gas for 300 miles!"

6. Be selective. Billboard companies generally want you to rent multiple locations. You get losers along with the winner you want. It's also very expensive. On the other hand, you might have the opportunity to buy a single billboard—one that stares prime prospects in the face. If you find it, buy it! Otherwise, consider other outdoor alternatives.

Billbored? Go beyond billboards!

Billboards are the most prominent form of outdoor advertising. But don't overlook other types of outdoor advertising covered in this chapter and elsewhere. For example, consider ads on and inside buses, trains, taxis, walls, sidewalk kiosks, clock faces, banners, park benches to name a few. Any of these might meet your needs for less cost than billboards.

Turn vehicles into billboards

Every car, truck and van you operate should be a mobile billboard that always sells! Your fleet may cover thousands of miles—daily—and scores of potential customers may see your vehicles. So cover them with big, bold, beautiful graphics.

Are you a florist? Blanket the van with flowers from top to bottom, front to back. Bakery? How about full color taste tempting treats! Even use your personal car. Take advantage of removable magnetic signs or rooftop illuminated signs like Domino's Pizza or Pizza Hut.

Park 'billboards' in prominent places

Sometimes you have to park your rolling billboards. Pick the most visible and busy locations. If your business is out of the way, cut a deal with someone on a heavily used road. Do you suffer from tough sign ordinances?

Paint up an old truck and park it where you'd like a sign. Are there times when your vehicles sit idle? Again, make deals with friends and others to park a vehicle on their premises for a few days—and you'll have mobile billboards citywide.

License plate and bumper billboards

Vanity or personality license plates are a good little billboard—if you can fit a super short message on your plate. If you can't, supplement your plate with a sticker or lettering on your bumper. For example, a free lance writer might have a plate that reads "EDIT IT" and lettering right under the plate that says "Free lance writer 585–8687." Over time thousands of prospects will see your ad message—and just one response could pay for the lettering and the personality plate fee.

Bumper stickers remind, reinforce

Bumper stickers are a cheap way to keep a name or simple message in the public eye. They remind or reinforce and work best in combination with other promotional efforts. Classic examples are "Jones for Council" or "Say no to drugs!" But you can use stickers to build traffic with messages like "Get FREE KEY with purchase at Jones Hardware."

Regardless of the message, stickers only work when displayed on a large number of vehicles—which most small businesses don't have. An alternative is to distribute your stickers to employees, customers, friends and family. Or run a contest in which people can win prizes for displaying your sticker. Tie-ins with other businesses are also useful, especially a newspaper, radio or TV station.

Make your sticker easy to read on a car bumper. Try to stay under five words. Use a big, bold plain typeface like Helvetica bold. Dark letters on a light background are easiest to read.

Exterior signs and banners

Good exterior signage is essential to any business but especially to those that depend on drop–in traffic. Start by having the largest, most visible permanent identification signs permitted by local ordinances.

Go for quality—your sign may be the first and only thing potential customers know about you. Make your first impression impressive!

Effective signs are clear, concise, easy to read and understand. Look at the signs used by national companies such as Exxon, Ford, GM or Holiday Inn hotels. Learn from their experience. Illuminate your signs so they attract attention and sell even when you are closed.

During sales and other special events, supplement your permanent signs with temporary banners and signs. Once again, go for quality. Avoid amateur signs that hurt your image. Sell with clear, concise messages displayed in large bold type on a light background.

Budget banners give big bang for buck

Banners have come a long way in recent years. The old oil cloth banners with painted letters are still around. But now you can purchase vinyl banners with computer generated letters for as low as $25 for a big 10' by 14" banner. One source is Kinko's Instant Signs. Call 800–443–9543. Also check franchise sign outlets. These sign specialists often offer same–day sign and lettering service as well as low prices.

Low–cost changeable message banner

A banner called the Build–A–Banner lets you change your message over and over again in minutes by slipping letters into clear plastic pockets. These outdoor and indoor changeable banners are great for promoting weekly or even daily specials. A Build–A–Banner would be ideal when preparing a new one–use sign each time would be too costly. For example, prices start at $195 for a basic 2' x 4' sign that comes with 160 letters, numbers, symbols and punctuation marks. Call Total Performance Co. of Dallas, Texas at 800–858–6825.

Transit shelters and benches

This medium consists of advertising panels on bus, trolley or train stop shelters and platforms. Areas without bus shelters often have benches on which ads are painted. Transit stop advertising generally isn't cheap or offbeat but can be if used selectively.

Shelter and bench ads work by reminding people about a product, business or event. They are most effective when deployed with other promotions. However, a unique, cost efficient advantage is the ability to buy specific geographic areas and even individual locations.

Target carefully. Capitalize on location flexibility. For instance, you can reach prospects on their way to shop. A store hidden in an office building could advertise on a shelter near the entrance. You could also buy a shelter directly outside a competitor's doorway.

Shelter impact depends on design as well as location. Some shelters are nothing more than a small roof held up by a two–sided ad box at either end of the "shelter." Others are elaborate four–sided structures which thoroughly protect patrons from the elements.

In the deluxe shelter, only waiting people will see the inside ads. The outside panel, however, is ideal for reaching pedestrians. If large enough, it also hits passing motorists—unless the panel faces the wrong way on a one–way street.

Similarly, bench ads generally are too small for passing motorists to read. They work well for transit patrons and pedestrians. Even so, people sitting on the bench may temporarily obscure or hide your message.

Hit the streets if you are considering a shelter or bench campaign. Personally walk up to and drive by every location you are contemplating. See how parked trucks, waiting passengers, building shadows, etc. affect your spots. Once underway, check actual ad placement. Make sure you have the exact location and panels you paid for. If not, get a free correction showing. Remember, think selectively.

Auto sunshades—deploy strategically

Auto sunshades have become popular in recent years because they are cheap and big enough for a good size message. Most businesses sell sunshades at low cost or give them to clients and prospects. That's fine but think strategically to get more from sunshades.

If you have a retail shop, for example, give them free to people who park nearby on a regular basis. People who have parking contracts, perhaps at a next door lot, are perfect. You'll now have scores of billboards reminding passers by about your business. Place one in your windshield and park in front of your business. It's a great way to circumvent local zoning restrictions. Or park at a big public event, on a busy street or in front of a competitor! Another strategy is to give them to employees and others who park near a prospect or business you are trying to influence.

To get the most from sunshades, come up with a sales message of six or less words. Have it printed in huge, sans serif black or bright red type on both sides—you'll promote to the public and the user at all times.

Highway directional and logo signs

Many states restrict or prohibit commercial signs such as billboards on major highways. But some let you advertise on standardized message boards that advise motorists of services available at the next exit. They are often called "logo signs" because you can include your business name and logo for a fee of around $1,500 annually. Ads actually appear on four signs: Two on the road itself and on two directional signs at the end of the exit ramps.

Logo boards are ideal for smaller businesses because all logos and names are the same size—which gives small local businesses the same impact as big national chains. Logo signs, however, are generally limited to gas, food, lodging and camping facilities. Many states also provide free signs for tourism services at exits. Call your state highway or transportation department about various sign programs.

Transit vehicle ads pinpoint

Ads in and on buses, streetcars and commuter trains are two totally different sales channels. And both can be quite expensive. Fortunately, you can cut costs sharply by buying space only on routes that reach your prime prospects. If you have goods or services that appeal to transit patrons, interior ads may fit your needs.

The average transit rider takes a 22 minute trip and does it 24 times a month. The rider also is "captive" with little else to do. So your ad can be seen over and over.

Interior transit ads are generally 11 inches high by 28 inches long which means your message must be short. Present a brief message along with your address and telephone number. If possible, include a take–one card or coupon. Call your local transit system marketing department for details.

Exterior transit ads are basically rolling billboards and should be treated accordingly in terms of appearance and content (see billboard tips elsewhere). They keep your name or product in the public eye. They are also effective for reaching people along a specific transit route—provided it is served by vehicles dedicated to that route. Other options include ads on downtown shopper shuttles, senior dial–a–ride services, apartment complex shuttles and special services.

Movable marquees grab attention

A movable marquee or portable reader board in front of your establishment will literally demand attention from passing pedestrians and even motorists. These signs get your message noticed because of their large size and flashy lights.

You can purchase a sign or rent one by the month. Either way, first check local ordinances. Also make sure you have enough sidewalk room for your intended sign. You can double your geographic exposure by cutting a deal with someone who has a good location elsewhere—you both rent double–sided boards and simply advertise on one side of each other's sign.

You may also know someone with a great location who won't rent a sign. Offer to pay for it yourself—and give your associate one side in trade for the right to position your sign at the person's business.

Walking, talking signs

Remember sandwich board signs? They seem to appear only on naked cartoon characters nowadays. That's too bad since they create a lot of attention for little cost. Walking signs are also a good way to circumvent many local ordinances prohibiting stationary sidewalk signs.

Hire someone to parade around busy downtown streets with

your sign. Public events, street concerts, fairs, beaches and other opportunities are also perfect for your walking sign. Have your person give out flyers, samples or coupons and other traffic builders. Train your sign bearer to answer questions about your wares.

For added impact, dress your moving billboard in a costume and change your message frequently. Oh yes, find a friendly, outgoing individual—with good feet and a thick skin.

Sidewalk A–frame signs get noticed

A simple sidewalk A–frame sign outside your business can boost sales fast by grabbing the attention of pedestrians. Too often people walk past a place for years without noticing it is there. This is especially true in congested, visually cluttered urban districts. But a properly positioned sidewalk sign will make you stick out.

A–frames will deliver for anyone on a street with good pedestrian traffic. If you offer daily specials or deals that change frequently, pick up a chalkboard sign. Go for height since parked vehicles can block your sign. To avoid legal problems, use common sense when you position your sign.

Sports signs add you to team

Ad signs at sports fields are reminders for products or services that appeal to fans. Pro level signs are pricey and probably wrong for smaller businesses. But high school, little league and other grassroots signs might be right for neighborhood-oriented businesses. They may also fit if you need to be identified with the community. By advertising you are cheering for the local favorite—a distinct edge when you deal with like–minded prospects.

T–shirts: Ads people proudly wear!

Incredible numbers of people gladly wear and even pay for T–shirts selling someone else's business or cause. Whether wet or dry, they draw attention. T–shirts keep your name or message in the public eye—often for years—or help publicize a special event.

T–shirts are also useful for boosting employee morale or as inexpensive uniforms. And they are unbeatable as sales incentives or giveaways. After all, the recipient receives a nice premium or gift while you get a longtime free walking billboard. For maximum impact, always buy quality T–shirts people will wear regularly for years. Come up with a sales message of eight words or less and have it printed in big, bold easy to read type on both sides of the T–shirts.

More body billboards!

T–shirts aren't the only way to use your body, or at least the upper half, as a billboard to promote your business. Jackets, sweat shirts, hats and shirts also help you promote in a crowd. Jackets and hats, along with T–shirts, are great for teams or organizations you sponsor. While you're at it, don't forget to hit below the belt. If your name is short enough, consider displaying it on shorts and swimsuits.Where is up to you.

Where to wear body billboards

Wear your walking billboards to trade shows, public events and anywhere else you might encounter prospects—and don't dismiss seemingly improbable opportunities. For example, I play basketball several days a week and always wear a T–shirt that reads "Increase your sales at low cost—ask me how." This beat up old $12 T–shirt has generated many marketing projects. Bottom line: Why pay big bucks for fashion garb promoting some other company when you can promote yourself?

Bagboards bag prospects

All your bags and boxes should sell. Print your name on them in the largest type that space permits. Use both sides on bags and all sides on boxes. Big, bold black type on a white or light background provides maximum visibility.

A dramatic splash of red or another loud color will help if used carefully. Forget frilly designs, logos, artsy colors, little stickers and other cute things people can't see or read anyway.

You want powerful mini moving billboards—readable across the street, shopping mall concourse, parking lot, trade show hall. If you add your name and phone number, place it in a corner where it won't obscure your name's readability.

Buttons good 'ask me' tool!

Buttons are a cheap way to prompt customers to ask about special offers or programs employees might forget to mention. They can also start conversations that allow employees to sell other products or services. Tailor your buttons to specific specials or use a general button that reads "Ask me about today's great special!" Buttons are also handy for employee sales contests and morale building drives. Ad specialty houses sell custom and generic buttons.

You can also purchase do–it–yourself button machines. With one of these you can make buttons as you need them. It's a fast, affordable way to have new buttons every week to promote various specials and deals. Call ad specialty houses for details.

Advertise in hotel rooms

Many hotels and motels accept in–room advertising from non–lodging businesses in the area. Many also permit delivery of food such as pizza, beverages and other items of interest to guests. If appropriate, look into this possible source of business. This approach is ideal for the many small motels that don't have their own eating facilities. While you're at it, remember to lavish desk clerks with freebies and other considerations so they will refer guests to your business when they need a service that you provide.

As for your own establishment, don't forget tent cards and other table or counter top promotional mediums. It's a common but effective way to sell more to existing customers and to promote new goods and services.

Provide a customer bulletin board

Put up a bulletin board for your customers. It's a good way to attract more traffic and to build client goodwill. It doesn't hurt to promote your own products and services on your board—many of your customers may read the bulletin board more than they read in–store sales signs.

Actively encourage people to post material on your bulletin board to keep it interesting—and well read. At the same time, you might want to limit your board to charities and other worthwhile causes. As for commercial operations, charge them for the space or barter for their goods and services—or work out a cross promotion.

9

Teleselling tips to ring up sales

How to make Yellow Pages pay

The Yellow Pages offer two irresistible advantages: (1) Most homes have one and (2) people who look there are ready to buy. That's why so many businesses advertise in the Yellow Pages. But that doesn't mean you should. Here are some pointers to help you decide:

1. When to use. You can benefit from a Yellow Pages ad when you are reasonably sure your prospects look there for your goods and services—or when you can steal customers from larger, established competitors. To do this, run a huge display ad and that makes your business look as substantial as your competition.

2. When to pass. Don't waste money on the Yellow Pages if your clients normally learn about you in other ways. And save your money if the Yellow Pages will produce more business than you can handle properly. Too much business is a happy problem—but one nonetheless. It could ruin a hard–earned reputation for service.

3. Avoid the worst mistake! NEVER tell customers in your other ads to get your telephone number from the Yellow Pages—you send them straight to the competition. Refer them instead to the White Pages. Better yet, include your telephone number in your ads.

4. Get proper coverage. Determine where your customers are likely to come from. Advertise in telephone books that blanket your target areas. If you market nationally, use Yellow Pages in all appropriate cities including those where you don't have offices. Don't overlook Business to Business Directories. Select multiple headings. Run a listing under every conceivable heading where prospects are likely to look for services or products like yours.

5. Track results. Always ask all callers how they heard about you. Instruct Yellow Pages readers to ask about a free prize offer or for a specific person. You can also install a special telephone line that's listed only in the Yellow Pages.

If you have multiple–line phones, list your last telephone line number in the ad. Lastly, remember telephone books list names alphabetically. Businesses heavily dependent on the Yellow Pages may want to rename themselves "A Whatever" to catch prospects who browse alphabetically. See later tip.

Hints for more productive ads

1. Increase your visibility. The obvious way is to buy a display ad since they outdraw standard line listings. If you can't afford one, try a boldface type listing. They are twice as effective as plain ones. Even a simple box around your ad will increase its visibility. Or use bullets to make services and products pop out from your ad. Colors like red in display ads can be very effective but you'll pay accordingly. On the other hand, color definitely helps smaller ads while not adding that much to your overall cost.

2. Include everything. Many people assume you don't sell or service items that are not listed in your ad. So include everything in your ad. An appliance store, for example, should list every brand it sells so anyone looking for a specific brand will know you carry it. Well–known logos are a must.

3. Hit hot buttons. You have to catch the roving eye. So make sure your headline includes your key benefit.

4. Be thorough. Include everything your potential customer must know to deal with you. Provide full name, address, directions, credit card and check policy, telephone numbers, hours of operation, parking.

'A' puts you at head of the list

Many prospects start at the top of the list when they look at names under a Yellow Pages heading. In fact, some people only call the first three or four names listed under a heading—which means companies buried in the middle are frequently ignored! So if you depend heavily on the Yellow Pages for business, start your company name with an A.

Either add an A to your existing name or change your name to a word that starts with the letter A. For example, Reliable Plumbing could call itself "A Reliable Plumbing," "A–1 Plumbing" or "Always Reliable Plumbing."

Generate green from White Pages!

The White Pages are truly the Cinderella of the telephone book world. They perform all the grunt work and are heavily used. Yet they are overlooked by many marketers. To use this valuable sales tool for all it is worth, follow these guidelines:

1. Do your homework. Make sure you get the basic White Pages listing to which you are entitled. Double check your name, address and telephone number.

2. Stand out! Consider upgrading your basic listing if you don't advertise in the Yellow Pages. Try bold face capital letters, super large bold face letters, rules, color and other options offered by your local telephone company.

3. Be easy to find! If you have a tricky name, buy cross listings. For instance, a restaurant named La Place should list under La Place, Place and Laplace.

4. Use the right books. Make sure you are in all the books your prospects use. If you are unsure about which books are appropriate, ask your telephone sales representative for help.

Review coupons, special directories carefully

Directory coupons are attractive but their value depends on your business. As for special directories, many are not well distributed. So hold off for now unless you find an unusual opportunity. Always ask for circulation statistics and then do your own research. Call customers, friends, and so forth—ask whether they ever use the directory you are considering.

Direct connect with phone book prospects

Businesses that depend heavily on the Yellow Pages should check into a telephone company service variously called Custom Connect Tips or Quick Tips. These are numbers Yellow Pages readers can call for recorded advice about the heading's subject. The numbers appear in a box at the top of the heading.

Each box contains a special telephone number and four tips with touch tone codes. The consumer dials the number and one of the codes to get advice about the heading's subject. You can sponsor these tips which means prospects learn about you when they want help or information before buying something. Additionally, the fact that you sponsor consumer advice suggests you are an authority and leader in your field.

Add low–cost 800 number

Many phone companies and long distance services now allow you to put an 800 number on an existing line for a small monthly fee and a per–call charge. Consequently, you can offer prospects and customers the same convenience, service and access as larger competitors—at a cost based strictly on actual usage. You don't need any special equipment or hook-ups. You can also customize your coverage area to reduce your expense. Contact phone companies for details.

Three ways to dial for dollars

The budget disadvantaged should definitely try telephone sales or "telemarketing." Calling is cheaper and less time consuming than direct sales or canvassing. It is also more flexible than direct mailings. You can tailor your message to the listener, deal with objections as raised—and close the sale on the spot. Best of all, you know immediately what works or doesn't and can take instant corrective action.

Telemarketing can be done in three ways (1) by you and your staff, (2) with a computer that dials and plays a recorded message or (3) through an outside telemarketing company. Computer calls annoy many people but still work well for some businesses. Professional telemarketers charge by the call or hour and should be considered. Before spending any money, make your own test sales calls. You'll have a rough benchmark to measure their results—you may also find your product or service can't be sold over the phone.

Time–tested telemarketing sales tips

If you decide to use telemarketing to any extent, you might start with these tips:

1. Work from a short outline. List on a single page the

important sales benefits, features and any other major points you want to cover.

2. Be yourself. Talk as you normally do. You'll sound more sincere. Use short, clear sentences. And smile—people claim they can sense it in someone's voice and attitude. Remember telephone etiquette. No gum chewing, eating and smoking while talking.

3. Prepare a detailed script for employees inexperienced in telephone sales. Write down exactly what you want your callers to say—and make them follow the script word for word. Continually refine through experience. Beef up what sells, delete stuff that doesn't. Use a script or outline but never let inexperienced employees free lance!

4. Make contact, present, close! Open with a genuinely warm, enthusiastic greeting. Try to establish a personal link with the prospect . . . comment on the weather, a local event, something you know about your party. Follow with questions requiring a yes answer.

This process involves the prospect and starts a positive dialogue. Make questions lead into your product or service. Then hit key benefits, features. Close by specifically asking for the sale or whatever else you want the person to do.

5. Objections are opportunities. They give you an opening to showcase your offering. If existing service satisfies a prospect, a good sales person responds with: "That's great. If you like X, you'll love our new X that provides better benefits for the same price." Anticipate objections and prepare possible responses.

6. Make callbacks. Telephone sales is demoralizing. People slam down phones, insult you. Rejection is constant, especially for cold calls. But you'll win some sales. You'll also find prospects who might buy in the future. Keep detailed call records—and develop a plan for calling back later.

7. Telemarketing works best with other sales efforts. For instance, send out a mailing and advise recipients you will be calling. Or instruct them to call about a secret sale, etc. for important customers.

You may conclude telemarketing is not for you. But guess what? You are already doing it—every time you or an employee gives price and product information to someone who calls your place of business. So take steps to make sure the job is done right.

Supply employees with scripts to help them answer telephone inquiries in a sales–directed manner. Once you and your employees get the swing of it, start placing calls to prospects—instead of hoping and waiting for them to call you.

Return ALL phone calls

You may be thinking "what kind of tip is this?" After all, it's so obvious. But the reality is many people don't return all their phone calls these days—and think nothing of it.

The practice used to be limited mainly to unsolicited sales calls. Now it's spreading to telephone calls in general. Most perpetrators excuse their behavior by rationalizing, "I didn't ask them to call me. Besides, I'm too busy . . . so why bother?" Besides being rude, ignoring phone calls hurts your sales in many ways. For starters, you create an enemy—someone who will probably go around bad mouthing you. Worse yet, you might miss a sales opportunity. After all, you'll never know how someone can help you now—or in the future—unless you talk with them.

Conduct a telephone sales blitz

A sales blitz is an intense, onetime undertaking in which a sales team tries to contact as many potential customers as possible in a short time period. The team can use telemarketing or face–to–face sales calls. As for the team, it can consist of professional sales people or employees and others specially trained for the occasion. The key advantage of a blitz is you rapidly generate the amount of sales that normally would take many months to develop. You can also run a blitz anytime but is most effective when you have a hook or message.

Good hooks include new or remodeled facilities, new products, people or services and new programs. An effective blitz demands strong planning. Decide exactly what's to be accomplished, duration (usually two or three days), where, who to contact. Developing a theme also helps. For example, "winter sales spectacular." Additionally, prepare a script for all participants and consider awarding prizes to team members who reach blitz goals.

Phone headsets raise sales productivity

A headset could raise the productivity of anyone who spends several hours a day on the phone. First forget old stereotypes. Headsets are now compact, comfortable, easy to use and offer sound quality rivaling handset phones. Some also cost less than $50. But they can benefit sales people, customer service representatives, busy executives and telephone operators.

A headset frees your hands to do other things while on the phone. It's also easier to move around, look up information and perform calculations. You spend less time just picking up and putting down the phone. A headset also reduces questions and errors by cutting out a lot of distracting background noise. Best of all, headsets constantly remind telemarketers what they are paid to do. Some males and supervisors may balk at wearing headsets. Don't worry about bruising their egos. Once they try headsets, they'll wonder how they ever did without them.

Give home phone number as VIP perk

Give your home telephone number to new customers and key clients. And let them know you only give it to close friends and associates. Then tell them they are free to call you anytime. Chances are they won't. But they'll feel special because of your gesture. As an added touch, hand write your number on your card when you give it to your client.

Soothe, sell to on–hold callers

Placing your customers on hold is bad for business but not always avoidable. Many callers simply hang up while others become disgruntled. Use the time instead to benefit both you and your customers. Replace your current radio station or silence with an upbeat, informative sales message. You'll win sales because a recent study found nearly 75% of callers stay on the line when offered a good on–hold advertising message.

Stress benefits—give on–hold callers summaries of new products, services and ways to use them more effectively. Promote special sales, offers and other interesting events.

To get started, contact your local telephone company marketing department or a firm that specializes in caller on–hold services. They can also furnish the simple tape player that automatically plays your message while callers are holding. It's easy to use and improves customer service and sales.

Unlock your voice mail jail

Admit it . . . don't you go nuts when you're stuck in someone's automated phone answering system and voice mail maze? After all the hassle, you feel like taking your business elsewhere. Or you leave an E–mail message only to receive a response a week later—if ever! Is that what you do to prospects? Whatever you do, don't let your voice mail become an electronic dead letter office. Get into the habit of checking for messages at least several times a day. And then discipline yourself to return all calls promptly. You'll put the electronic revolution to work for you—instead of against you.

Check out voice mail sales options

Too many small businesses treat voice mail as a sophisticated answering machine or secretarial substitute and overlook the sales potential. An obvious first step is to get a beeper. Paging services now provide any geographical coverage you want. You can also choose from tone or voice paging, numeric display or message displays several pages long.

Some voice mail services also offer 800 numbers for a low monthly fee and a time usage charge. It's a low–cost way to provide customers and prospects nationwide with an around the clock toll–free number for messages and placing orders. You can then process them at your convenience.

Be different: Have human answer phone!

Human contact creates a personal reason for customers to patronize you rather than competitors. What's more, many prospects want to deal with a person. That's human nature. As more businesses go to voice mail, you can create your own exclusive market niche by retaining the human touch.

Commit to having your callers reach a person first. If it's necessary to leave a message, give the caller a choice between giving it to a person or leaving it on voice mail. If you don't have a staff, consider an answering service. Many charge as little as $50 per month including the first 125 messages and around 25¢ per call after that. They also offer call forwarding and paging options.

10

Direct mail magic that makes money!

What direct mail can do for you

Direct mail is potentially your most cost efficient marketing vehicle on a cost–per–sale basis. The reason is you can choose exactly who receives your advertising mailer. Additionally, you control timing, mailing size and cost.

Above all, **accountability is absolute.** Unlike other mediums, you know precisely how many pieces you mailed, what you paid, sales results and exact cost per sale.

Direct mail also fits today's life-styles. Busy prospects can read direct mail when they like. There's no sales pressure, no hassle. In this relaxed setting, you can walk prospects through your entire sales presentation. Use whatever words, pictures, techniques and situations you want. You control the content—totally.

But successful direct marketing takes a lot of know how—and even when you do everything right, you generally can expect just a one or two percent return at best. But don't let that scare you! The fact is direct mail is a highly established science. What works and doesn't is generally well known. Here are some basic time–tested and proven principles you should follow if you try direct mail:

10 ways to boost direct mail results!

1. Pick your target carefully. As in all promotional activities, the first step is to determine exactly who you want to reach. Clearly define your target audience so you can be as specific as possible when you undertake the next steps.

2. Pinpoint your BIG benefit. Your product or service may offer many benefits to your target prospects—but there is only one BIG benefit! Find the one thing that is most important to your target audience.

3. Find the best possible prospect list. Always start with your own customer lists and accounts. Next check the free resources described elsewhere in this book. You can also buy commercial lists of people who already have or are likely to respond to offers like yours.

4. Check rented lists carefully. If you buy or rent lists, check compilation and revision dates since lists become outdated rapidly. A good list source is the *Direct Mail List Rates and Data* directory published by the Standard Rate & Data Service. Available at many libraries, this directory contains over 100,000 mailing lists.

An option is to hire a list broker. You pay no more but get professional help. Hacks exist, however, so check their references carefully.

5. Make your envelope sell. Everything rests on the instant your prospect eyes the envelope—but it doesn't have to be fancy or expensive to get opened.

A proven way to get your mail opened is to promise a benefit on the envelope. Words like "free," "sale," "limited time offer" and "bargain" sound trite but are time tested! You can promise a free sample, a free test or a specific benefit. For example, you can say "in just five minutes, we'll show you how to increase your production!"

6. Start your letter with a headline! Open your letter with a one or two line headline that describes your BIG benefit and what action you want prospects to take. You can even ask for an order in your headline. In any case, always use a headline because studies show most people only read headlines.

7. Clear, complete information essential. Restate your BIG benefit in the first and last paragraphs because that's the only part of a letter many people read. As you go along, include all the information prospects need to make a buying decision. State benefits clearly. Remember people hate to read—make your letter effortless. Hold sentences under 14 words. Use three sentences per paragraph. Showcase key benefits with underlining, bold type, indents or a second color.

8. Ask for the sale After you have made your sales presentation, ask for the order in clear, unmistakable terms. Include a separate ready–to–use order form—it boosts sales!

9. Make it easy to order. Tell readers exactly what they must do to buy your product or service. Anything you do to make placing an order easier will improve your results. Tell prospects you accept credit cards, take checks. Add an 800 number, 24 hour service.

10. End with a postscript. Nearly everyone reads those two or three little lines at the end of a letter! Restate your major benefit. Reinforce it with a reason to act now. Offer a free gift, a discount, a free sample or some other limited time offer. Like the headline, the postscript should entice prospects to read your entire letter.

Hand addressing highly effective!

A direct mail study found most people open envelopes that look official or look like bills. It didn't say how they felt about being fooled but they probably weren't in a buying mood. On the other hand, most people open window envelopes or those that promise a free sample inside. If you can't afford either, here's something you can do that's honest and dirt cheap: The same study found most people open hand addressed envelopes—which makes this technique ideal for businesses with small mailings.

Stamp smarts that get mail noticed

Many people discard sales mail with preprinted bulk postage called "indicias." Even metered mail can be a turn off. But genuine stamps increase the odds your sales piece will be noticed and opened.

Using the real thing is easy since bulk rate as well as first class stamps are available in handy rolls. Other eye arresting tricks include bold, colorful special occasion stamps and lots of low denomination stamps. One four and five five–cent stamps will definitely grab attention. For smaller VIP mailings, consider elegant envelopes embossed with first class postage. It's an unusual touch for upscale offerings.

Whenever possible, mail first class. The cost premium is modest but lets you rubber stamp "first class" on your mail to make it look more important. You can also preprint "address correction requested." This service is free on first class mail under two ounces and helps you cut mailing costs while keeping your list current.

Test for best direct mail results!

Successful professional direct mailers never stop testing. They constantly tinker with every mailing component to see what sells best—and so should you. Before you do a big mailing, conduct small tests with 10 or 20 pieces. Test different offers in identical envelopes. Or test envelopes that have a different sales message on the outside but the same offer inside. You can also test different mailing lists, envelope sizes, ink color, letter appearance and other variables to see what's most effective for you.

Bypass bottom to speed mail

Never take a large mailing to your corner mailbox or even your local post office branch. Doing so generally slows down delivery and increases the likelihood of errors since more people must process it. To speed delivery, bring it to the most important postal facility in your area, usually the main post office.

Additionally, anything you do to facilitate handling, such as presorting by zip codes and bar coding, will shorten delivery time. Finally, religiously adhere to standard envelope sizes, addressing requirements and other basics. For details, pick up free guides available at most post offices.

Free start–up mailing list

Get a great start–up mailing list—free—by compiling the names of your current customers. Use your billing, sales and other records. Conduct a drawing or other giveaway to compile names and addresses. Process them on a personal computer. Otherwise, have the data typed on mailing label sheets that fit copy machines. Avery brand labels are available in many sizes at most office supply stores.

Free mailing lists in one big book

You already possess one of the world's best tools for building free mailing lists. This valuable tool separates businesses by categories. You can also use it to sort prospects by location. This great prize? Your local Yellow Pages or Business–to–

Business directory. All you have to add are zip codes. **Bonus:** The Postal Service will add zip codes to your list or correct them—free—if you give them your list on a floppy disk. Call your local Post Office for details.

Free public mailing lists

Depending on your product or service, you may be able to get sales leads from various public agencies. Check local, state and Federal agencies. The county clerk, town hall, courthouse and state motor vehicle office are great sources of free information. Births, weddings, divorces, deaths, home ownership, car registrations, bankruptcies and a wealth of information can be yours with just a little effort.

Frequency pays off

Don't mail to 10,000 prospects once a year. Send to 2,000 five times a year. Frequency builds familiarity, confidence—and acceptance. The response rate will rise accordingly.

Coupon mailing services

Commercial coupon mailing services often are cheaper and more effective than doing it yourself. Services save you money by producing and distributing your coupons with those of others. You can also target specific geographic areas, usually of about 10,000 homes. And most cities have several services you can find under Advertising—Direct Mail in the Yellow Pages. But make sure you get what you pay for by asking tough questions.

What to look for: Ask about **delivery timeliness.** Most coupon packages are sent by bulk mail and delivery is unpredictable. This could cause problems for time sensitive offers. **Delivery accuracy.** Will packets reach the promised homes?

Ask for what is called "postal certification" that confirms the mailing was made as promised. Check out **exclusivity**. Will you be the only business of your kind in the mailing? If not, reconsider. Finally, inspect the actual **mailing package.** Do you think your prospects will open it? Would you?

Post Card decks

Post card decks are groups of post cards mailed in a clear plastic package with each post card promoting a different product or service. Interested prospects either return your post card or call a number on the card for more information.

The packages are assembled by professional mailers who handle all the mailing details and can furnish you with a huge variety of target mailing lists. They will also design and print your post card for you. The cost is usually around five to 10 cents per card which covers card production and mailing—the works. The minimum buy–in is generally $1,500.

Some participants report a response rate as high as 10% which makes the decks very cost effective despite the initial expense. Once again, your offer is the key. Offers typically include a special discount or some free incentive. For a complete list of card deck suppliers, see the *Direct Mail List Rates and Data* directory published by Standard Rate & Data Service. Most major libraries have a copy.

On the other hand, card deck mailers may approach you to participate and brag about how good they are. If that's the case, offer to participate on a per lead or per order basis.

Form your own cooperative mailing

Another way around high mailing costs is to organize your own cooperative mailing. If you are in a mall, try to get your mall association to do it. Or form your own co–op by contacting friends, associates, suppliers and other compatible businesses. Pool costs and mailing lists. Parties reluctant to give out confidential lists don't have to. Let them apply their labels to the completed mailing packages. They then mail the items, thereby protecting their names.

Personal letters reach top prospects

A direct mail campaign in which you send personal letters to prime prospects costs little but works remarkably well. The reason is most people open and read letters that look personal.

First learn all you can about your best prospects. Look for things in common like colleges, clubs, cars, hobbies, interests and shared experiences. Next write a truly personal letter—not simply a "personalized" letter with the prospect's name in the opening and body. Blend in your sales message. Finally, use your personal name on the envelope—and add a real postage stamp as the final touch.

If you don't get a response in 10 days, call or send another personal letter and keep it short. Restate your sales points and refer to your earlier letter. If that fails, make third and fourth efforts! You are building familiarity—and people patronize firms with which they are familiar.

11

How to use premiums without pain!

When to use coupons, other premiums

FREE! It may be the most powerful word you can use in advertising or promotion. And not far behind is SAVE! No wonder so many businesses of all sizes use premiums, coupons and other incentives to stimulate sales.

Sales incentives are best used to attract first–time buyers, create repeat traffic and entice customers to purchase more than they planned. For example, coupons are a good way to attract people who may be unfamiliar with your business. And they are ideal to promote a new product, service or location.

Premiums can give sales edge

Sales incentives such as premiums can also give you an edge in some situations. A premium is an item you give away free or at a discount to encourage potential customers to buy your main offering. Premiums are often vital to your sales because the right premium can be your decisive edge when consumers believe you and your competitors offer identical products and services. Or when they feel any differences are irrelevant.

The ideal premium ties in with your business, is easy to promote and has perceived or real value far greater than your cost. Examples include a free oil change with a tune–up, baseball cap and bat days. The only limit is your imagination.

Premiums also help you avoid price cuts. When under pressure to reduce prices, see if you can add a premium to enhance the attractiveness of your basic product or service—without lowering the normal price. The right premium might generate enough new sales to cover the additional cost.

Finally, sales incentives are often a competitive necessity—if everyone else is giving away coupons or premiums, you may be forced to do the same thing. Bottom line? Consider sales incentive options when you face one of the above situations.

How to use them properly

Make no mistake! Coupons, premiums and other incentives are price cuts. You can waste money by giving discounts to clients who would otherwise pay full price. Some customers also stop buying when the incentives end. Keep these points in mind to minimize your risk:

1. Anyone can reduce prices. Reducing your price is an admission you can't sell your product or service on the basis of its intrinsic value alone.

2. Increase value before you cut! Look for ways to give your customers more for the same price. Try to improve quality, quantity, appearance, service or market position. For example, a snack bar could offer a free beverage with the purchase of a sandwich platter rather than a plain sandwich.

3. Slash prices with a purpose. Set definable goals for your cut. Say "attract 10 new corporate accounts by December 15" rather than "attract corporate accounts."

4. Set a deadline. Make prospects feel they must act now to avoid missing a great opportunity. Depending on your business, three or four weeks is usually ample time.

5. Build for the future. Forget flighty one timers and bargain hunters. Develop incentives that encourage new customers to try you several times, not just once. It's trite but true—people are loyal to businesses with which they are familiar. Here are coupon and discount programs that meet these objectives:

Repeat coupons build return business

Using coupons to induce sampling or first–time patronage is common. But many businesses forget return coupons can generate repeat business and long–term loyalty. Plan carefully to avoid discounting existing repeat business (although it's smart to reward current good customers to retain them).

A basic strategy is to distribute several coupons at once. Each is redeemable at a specific time, such as once a month. The idea is to get the prospect into the habit of patronizing your business. Another approach is to give your customer a future trip coupon when completing the current transaction. Either way, customers have a specific reason to return.

Coupon to entice impulse buyers

Businesses that depend on impulse buyers should coupon heavily since studies show coupons encourage impulse buying. In fact, one source asserts that 25% of shoppers buy products they don't need immediately—just to take advantage of coupon savings. Psychology is also at work since many people use coupons because it makes them feel smarter. After all, everyone likes to believe they outsmarted the seller!

Start a frequent buyer program

Airline frequent flyer programs build customer loyalty and repeat business. You can set your sales flying with a frequent buyer program. Develop a simple point system that results in various prizes. Aim the program at the actual individuals—not necessarily bosses—who make final buying decisions or selections. A hotel, for instance, would target secretaries who make hotel reservations for a company's visitors.

Select widely popular prizes that offer instant gratification such as dinner for two at a popular restaurant, fruit or wine and cheese baskets, a big–name perfume, a pizza party and anything else you can barter. Send out a monthly flyer that lists point balances and available prizes.

Customer discount cards build loyalty, sales

Discount cards, unlike one–shot coupons, are intended for repeat use until completed or expiration. You can sell or give discount cards to potential customers. One approach is to hand out discount cards to loyal customers for free while charging everyone else.

To get more exposure, donate discount cards to churches, schools and other organizations for fund raisers. Consider printing customized coupons with the group's name. Also, let groups keep receipts from card sales or donate cards as door prizes. The idea is to motivate groups to generate publicity, goodwill and sales for you.

Give discount cards to contacts

Reward your contacts—and increase sales—by giving them discount cards they can sign and distribute to their employees. These cards give your contacts a new employee perk that doesn't cost them anything. Send out 10 or so initially and invite your associates to call for more.

To achieve greater distribution, send the cards to major businesses and other targets. As for the cards, they can be one–shot deals or usable repeatedly during a specified time span.

Enhance the card's prestige by instructing the employer to type in the employee's name.

Always coupon at off–premise activities

Anytime you promote your business off premises, give people a concrete inducement to patronize your actual location. This is especially important if you participate in trade shows, fairs, exhibitions, booths at malls and charitable events.

Your sales tool can be a discount coupon, a free gift or a "completer." For example, offer a two–part gift. The potential customer receives one part at the show and the other at your business. Or give them a coupon at the show redeemable for a gift at your business. To build a mailing list, require prospects to fill out an address and information card.

Accept competitors' coupons

You may have a rival who is hurting you by saturating your trade area with coupons. Fight back by accepting the competitor's coupons! If you aren't distributing any coupons at the time, your competition will be doing it for you. Run a small newspaper ad stating you accept So & So's coupons and give an additional $1.00 discount or some other incentive. Small businesses can use this tip to compete with big national chains and franchises that coupon frequently.

Be first with gift certificates

Many businesses fail to offer gift certificates. And fewer still sell them year round. That's a shame on both counts since virtually every business can use them somehow to spark sales—it just takes imagination and maybe a sense of humor.

For starters, gift certificates are ideal for Christmas, graduations, birthdays, weddings, divorces, Bat and Bar Mitzvahs, christenings, confirmations, First Communions, friendships and more. Imagine being the first dry cleaners in your area to offer the gift of clean, odor–free clothes. Or the first florist that lets the recipient choose the flowers.

How about maid service for a week? Or dental care, car service, financial planning (ideal for newlyweds, college grads), health club lessons . . . everything from serious to gag gift. You can also sell gift certificates at a discount or exchange them with other businesses for use in contests and promotions.

12

Turn computer into desktop money maker

Why computer is marketing must

A basic desktop computer system will give you many of the more sophisticated marketing capabilities your bigger competitors possess. Even an entry level computer with simple software will let you produce effective flyers, brochures, ads, stuffers, proposals and other sales aids.

You can use the same setup to maintain mailing lists, analyze sales, generate labels, print form letters and perform other advanced marketing projects. You can make last minute changes to proposals and presentations—without creating a crisis. You also retain greater control since you reduce your dependence on outside vendors.

On top of all this, today's systems are more affordable, faster and easier to use than ever. **But be forewarned**— we haven't reached perfection yet. It still takes awhile to learn how to use the stuff. Until you do, the pace could be agonizingly slow and frustrating.

Yes, you will save money, especially by handling in house some tasks you now send out. But the savings will come in time, not in the beginning. Finally, the old saying "garbage in, garbage out" is as true today as ever. The world's best software can't help someone who doesn't know what communicates well or looks good!

Best computer for marketing

Technology and prices are changing rapidly so it's hard to discuss computer specifics and still be timely. Even so, the fundamentals remain the same. If you are starting from scratch, you will need a computer, video monitor (TV screen) and a printer. Useful options include a scanner to add pictures to your computer and a modem to "talk" via telephone to other modem–equipped computers.

Desktop computers fall into two groups: IBM PCs and their compatible friends and Apple's Macintosh. Both are fine but I personally find the Macintosh family easier to learn and operate. It's also ideal for desktop publishing, marketing jobs and other business tasks.

Nowadays Apple offers numerous computer models. A good buy for businesses with simple needs is the Performa 475. It comes with a color monitor, keyboard and a variety of software and sells for about $1,300. More advanced business users should consider the Quadra 630 series. Expect to pay $1,800 to $2,200 for a complete system.

If you have the money, step up to Apple's new generation of computers, the Power Macintosh. These computers are faster than most competing computers yet are simple to run and compatible with existing Mac software. The most affordable is the Macintosh Performa 6100 series. It sells for $1,800 to $2,800 depending on the accessories and memory.

Whatever you buy, acquire a system you can upgrade later. Above all, purchase far more memory and storage capability than you think you need—you always end up needing far more memory than you anticipated!

Nothing beats genuine laser printer

Looking good on paper is an essential part of a credible professional image—and nothing reproduces your computer creations better than a genuine PostScript laser printer.

PostScript laser printers deliver clear, crisp output other printers, such as inkjet printers, can't match. You can buy models that print with 300 dots per inch (dpi) quality for under $1,000 and better 600 dpi quality for around $1,400. All are suitable for day–to–day business and desktop publishing jobs.

Shopping tips: Compare page printing speed, memory, whether you can upgrade your memory, how they handle envelopes and odd paper sizes, paper capacity, special paper and envelope trays, ease of use, compatibility with your computer and, of course, price. Also investigate maintenance needs, supply costs, especially for toner, and warranties.

Want color? Quality color laser printers run $4,000 and up. But you can buy a color inkjet printer for under $500. It's a low–cost way to add a splash of color to presentations, overheads, proposals, reports and other documents. Good choices are Hewlett Packard's *DeskWriter 560C* and Apple's *StyleWriter 2400.* If you have the money, supplement your regular PostScript laser printer with a color ink–jet printer.

The best software for marketing

Your marketing efforts require specialized computer software. If you are just starting out, buy an integrated software package. These combine page layout and graphics design, word processing, spread sheets, charts, data bases, label making and telecommunications in a single bundle. Popular choices are *ClarisWorks, Microsoft Works* or *WordPerfect Works*. Integrated packages are a bargain compared to buying separate applications. They sell for $79 to around $199.

The graphics usefulness of integrated packages is somewhat limited. So you may also want to purchase a more sophisticated design package that includes easy to use templates and sample layouts. A good buy is *Aldus HomePublisher* at $49. *Aldus PageMaker* ($495) is for advanced designers and can handle complex desktop publishing and design jobs.

Managing your small business is a lot easier if you use the right accounting software. A package that stands out is *M.Y.O.B. 4.0.* It includes a general ledger, accounts receivable, accounts payable, payroll, inventory and many other basic needs and sells for around $110. The $45 *Quicken* package is ideal for home–based and super small businesses.

If you do a lot of mailings, look into *Bulk Mailer Plus.* This is a professional mailing list manager that includes POSTNET bar coding, ZIP+4 and other features necessary to give bulk mailers the best postal rates available. It sells for around $295. A simpler version for lighter applications costs $149.

Always shop around. You'll find that mail order houses generally sell software for less than computer stores. See ads in *MacUser* and *MACWORLD* magazines, two major Macintosh computer publications.

Bargain software for marketing

High–buck commercial software may be overkill for some of your needs. Before you spend, check out freeware and shareware. Freeware is software that the developers allow you to use for free. Shareware is software developers distribute on the honor system. They ask you to send them a fee, generally $2 to $40, if you use their software.

These bargain products are often well designed and offer many of the main features found in their expensive commercial counterparts. And you may not need the functions they lack anyway. There are budget programs for text editing, word processing, drawing, design, painting, clip art, spread sheets, telecommunications, time reminders, appointment books and other business–related applications. There are also many small programs called utilities to help you work faster and make your computer easier to use.

Budget software is available from local Macintosh user groups (call Apple Computer at 800–538–9696, ext. 500 for one near you), electronic bulletin board services and commercial companies that distribute shareware for a fee. Check ads in *MacUser* and *MACWORLD.* Bargain programs abound. Discuss your needs with experienced user group members and on–line service participants to find the best.

Sample good choices: *MattPaint*, a great little color painting program that's perfect for most simple graphic needs. Requested fee is just $15. *AppleDraw*, a free drawing program. *MiniWriter*, a $12 word processor. *Address Book*, a $30 address book that also prints on labels, envelopes, Rolodex cards or in a little booklet. *To Do!,* a $15 desk accessory that helps you keep track of your schedule and activities.

More for the frugal: *BiPlane*, a $59 spread sheet with power and sophistication rivaling some commercial products. *Mariner*, a $40 spreadsheet with comprehensive manual. *Disinfectant*, an excellent virus protection program that is free. *ZTerm*, an efficient and easy to use $30 telecommunications program for use with modems (see modem tip). *Compact Pro*, a $25 item that shrinks your computer files to save valuable memory space.

Color from black and white printers

Color sells—and you can get dazzling color and stunning designs from ordinary black and white printers by using preprinted multicolored forms.

You can buy letterheads, frames, messages, theme designs and mailers preprinted in a rainbow of colors. Choices include papers preprinted in top–to–bottom or corner–to–corner color gradations and multicolored designs. Just imprint your company name and sales message.

Especially useful are multicolored brochure forms preprinted on one or both sides. Some include scored, perforated Rolodex cards and reply/return cards to create powerful yet affordable mailers. Coordinated envelopes are another plus.

All these items are intended specifically for standard laser printers and office copiers. You can also use them in offset printing. Check local office supply stores for samples. Or call PaperDirect, Inc. at 800—272–7377 and BeaverPrints at 800—923–2837 for a free catalog. These companies offer a wide assortment of preprinted color forms and other clever promotional supplies for computer printers and copiers.

Computer presentations pack punch

Turn your desktop computer into a Hollywood studio—through new presentation software. With it, you can use color, graphics, even motion, sound and animation to create powerful sales presentations.

Preparing overheads and slides is a snap. But you can also develop elaborate "multimedia" presentations with color, sound and motion. You can then display your work on most available desktop and portable computers—or transfer your computer–created show to videotape for mailing and personal delivery.

If you have some desktop design experience, you can handle simple shows yourself. Leave more complicated presentations to pros. Cost? Basic software packages with graphics, type styling, chart and editing features run $50 to $500.

Animation and 3–D programs easily top $1,000. Even if you buy and use only entry–level products, you will be doing more than many of your competitors.

Scanners sell with pictures

Sometimes a picture is worth a thousand words. On those occasions, a scanner lets you add product illustrations, pictures and other eye–grabbing graphics to your computer creations. Even hand–held models that sell for around $300 are satisfactory for smaller graphics and basic applications.

The hand–held models are fine for line art, illustrations, clip art, type, handwriting—any flat image source. They can also reproduce photographs and half tones reasonably well. You can rotate, flip or resize your images. You can change contrast and brightness. You can also draw, erase, invert, sharpen, flip or rotate specific parts of your scanned image.

If serious desktop publishing is on your mind, buy a flatbed scanner. You have more model and feature choices. Scan quality is also better. A color flatbed scanner could be a smart choice since they cost roughly the same—around $1,000—as gray–scale flatbed scanners. You can work in gray–scale (black and white dot patterns that recreate shades of gray) for now and move up to color when you are ready.

Modems make right connections

A modem is a plain little box that lets your computer communicate via telephone with other modem–equipped computers. But unlike Pandora's box, this one holds good sales, research and convenience possibilities for you.

With a modem, you can exchange sales, technical and other information with clients and prospects. You can access numerous commercial information services like *America Online* and *CompuServe*. You can tap into computer user groups and electronic bulletin boards that cater to specific interests and professions. You can conduct research, check stock quotes, shop, make travel reservations and do a million other useful things. Yet modems are easy to hook up, operate and are more affordable than ever.

How to buy: Get the fastest, most accurate modem you can afford for your needs. You'll save time and money in long distance and online user fees. That's why modems are rated by how fast they send data with speed commonly expressed as bits per second (bps).

Basic 2,400 bps modems sell for as low as $75. But they are hopelessly slow when you access online services or communicate regularly with other computer users. Instead, buy a 14,400 bps data/fax/voice modem—you'll get a complete communications center for as low as $100. An excellent modem choice is the *Hayes ACCURA 144+FAX 144* which sells for $169. It's highly reliable, easy to use and comes with great software. Best of all, the manual is clearly written and ideal for beginners.

Modems that operate at 28,800 bps are becoming common and cost around $250—and are well worth the higher initial cost if you expect to access online services frequently.

Check compatibility: Whatever modem you consider, make sure it will work with your computer. The software you need usually comes with the modem but often is complicated. An easy–to–use bargain software alternative is *ZTerm*. This excellent shareware is available from local user groups, computer buffs and online services.

13

More business to business sales tips

Publish your own newsletter

If you are a service professional or sell to other businesses, consider publishing a free newsletter. It's a time–tested way to present yourself as an authority in your field at low cost.

A newsletter can also help you stay in touch with your customers. And you can turn it into a mailer or a handout promotional piece. Above all, the newsletter is a subtle and inoffensive way to remind indifferent potential customers about you. Here are some nuts and bolts:

Give readers specific news and benefits. Start by giving your readers timely, vital and interesting information about their field they can't get elsewhere. Focus on the meaning or impact of the news. Interpret events, trends, new products, services and technologies from your unique perspective—and explain what they mean to your readers. Offer tips, ideas and other practical ways to cash in on the latest developments.

Always sell! The newsletter's purpose is to make money for you. Constantly look for ways to subtly yet surely blend your products or services into stories. Tie events and developments to what you do. But don't be too obvious or heavy handed—few people will waste time reading a puff piece devoid of useful information.

Format and timing. When it comes to format, a successful newsletter can be as simple as a plain one–page sheet typed or prepared on a home computer. If you have a computer, add charts and other graphics. But send it out monthly—and certainly not less than quarterly. Anything less is too infrequent to have any meaningful impact.

Where to get newsletter help

If you don't have the time to write the whole newsletter yourself, there are many ways to get free stories. This includes news releases from your suppliers, trade association material, contributions by free–lance writers, guest columns by associates and especially stories and letters from your readers. You can also report what was said in other publications. Services offer generic newsletters to which you simply add your name, address and other localized information. See the Yellow Pages under News Publications. Some trade associations also provide form newsletters for their members.

Launch your own magazine

Many businesses are doing just that to drum up interest—and sales. We're not talking about the slick, four–color jobs that sell thousands of copies. Instead, many entrepreneurs are launching simple one color magazines that they print at the corner quick printer.

Quantities as low as 100 copies are common. As for content, the new mini magazines feature indepth stories of interest to their target readers. Mixed in are ads and stories about the publisher's services or goods. If you're a writer and designer at heart or have one in the family, consider your own magazine. It's a great creative outlet. Best of all, you can often publish and distribute one to prime customers and clients for less than the cost of a display ad in a major daily newspaper.

Fax newsletter novel and money saver

If a regular newsletter isn't right for you, consider a fax newsletter. Fax newsletters are still relatively rare—and could draw more attention than a printed publication. You can also include time sensitive and last minute information that would arrive too late if mailed.

A fax newsletter will also eliminate postage, printing and handling expenses. You can even sell ads in your fax newsletter to help pay for it. One caution: If you send faxes late at night, first check with your recipients. Some people have their fax machines on home phone lines—and won't be real happy to receive a fax from you at 3 am in the morning!

Start VIP fax 'Profit Alert!'

You can never do enough for your best customers. That's why a VIP fax "Profit Alert!" can pay off big!

Use it to rapidly and simultaneously advise key clients about new services, products and other hot opportunities. A travel agency, for example, could fax a weekly list of temporary travel bargains. Unlike the mail or personal telephone calls, you'll reach everyone within minutes and at about the same time—so you won't ruffle anyone's feathers.

Your fax cost should be offset by what you save on postage, printing and handling. For maximum impact, design a fax cover sheet that screams "Profit Alert!" in big, bold, impossible to ignore graphics.

Fax mail fast, cheap medium

Fax mail companies can now send a fax for you to thousands of recipients with just one telephone call by you. Fax mail is ideal for hot offers, new products and services—or any time you need fast delivery of information to many recipients. You also avoid postage, printing, stuffing and other mailing expenses. And you can choose names from your own database or those supplied by the fax mail service. In fact, many fax mail services maintain national as well as local databases. Check the Yellow Pages under Fax Transmission Service for fax mail services.

Add fax on demand service

Fax on demand lets you give prospects information exactly when they want it—seven days a week, 24 hours a day. Callers dial a special number. They then hear a menu of options for information about your offering. As soon as they hang up, a computer faxes them the information they requested. You can install your own system or hire a service bureau.

If you handle large numbers of routine information requests, fax on demand might be for you. For example, it's ideal for dealing with the flood of inquiries you receive after announcing a new product. Admittedly, some people don't like fax machines. Still, fax on demand gives most prospects information when they want it—and when they feel like buying.

Advertise on the information highway

Computer savvy businesses should promote themselves through bulletin board services, commercial on–line services and other channels that are emerging as you read this. Start with special interest bulletin boards or forums where you can contribute helpful information. In most instances, you can add information about your services, a telephone number or an E–mail address. Many technology and service companies are already finding new prospects in this way. E–mail also allows you to "chat" with potential customers.

14

Little tricks to create big–time image

Super small operations, home–based businesses and new start–ups share a discouraging problem—the fact that many prospects won't deal with what appears to be a shoestring operation. You don't want to lie but you have to project stability and trust like your bigger, more established competitors. Here are some ways to enhance your image—and avoid looking like a one–person band:

Cheap alternatives to home address

If your home address affects your credibility, you have several low–cost alternatives. A U.S. Post Office box is still a cheap yet effective way to avoid a home address. If you live in an apartment building, use the word suite instead of apartment in your address. Ask a friend or family member to let you use his or her business address and accept your mail. You can also acquire a real street address just about anywhere by renting a box at a private mailbox service. Here's how:

Rent a real address locally or worldwide

Perhaps you need a real street address across town, in a target market across the country—or on the other side of the world.

A low–cost solution is to rent a mailbox at one of over 2,500 Mail Boxes ETC. (MBE) centers in the U.S., Canada and worldwide. You can rent a box from them—with a real street address—for as low as $8 to $15 a month. As an option, you can add a phone with answering service and fax number.

You can secure an out–of–state address or establish "branch offices" nationwide or worldwide by renting MBE boxes in target areas. So you can appear local without the cost of a real local office or sales representative.

In addition to mail, MBE accepts packages and priority mail from UPS, FedEx and other private shippers. You can call MBE centers to see if you have mail—which they will forward to you for a charge. They also provide fax service, copying and 24–hour access to your mailbox. To find MBE locations worldwide, call 1–800–789–4623.

Join or register with BBB

New or smaller businesses can gain credibility fast by joining the Better Business Bureau. You'll have to meet certain standards and conditions you presumably want to uphold anyway. Membership entitles you to use the Bureau's name in your ads and establishment. If you can't afford to join, register by filling out their simple questionnaire. When people call about you, the Bureau can confirm you are registered and that there are no complaints about you. Which is a great free plug!

Chamber membership good for image

Join the local chamber of commerce to enhance your credibility. Membership implies you are a stable, established part of the community. You will also gain opportunities to network and promote your business. Be sure to include the chamber's name and, if permissible, logo in your sales material.

Testimonials build credibility

Testimonial letters can provide the credibility new small businesses often lack. Fortunately, they are frequently yours for the asking. The best time to ask a client for one is right after you successfully complete a job. If your customer is part of a larger company, ask them to send a letter of recommendation to other departments or branches. Some clients may want you to write the letter for them—so keep a draft handy. Use your testimonial letters in sales mailings, information kits and as handouts. If your office has a reception area, display your testimonial letters along with any awards you receive (see next tip).

Awards: Endorsements that sell

Awards, commendations and trophies are valuable third party endorsements of your work or expertise. If prospects come to your establishment, display your awards where everyone can see them. When somebody asks to see samples or proof of your skills, humbly point to your trophy collection. Others can toot your horn far better than you!

Don't be modest. Include everything you ever received all the way back to high school. The idea is to have a huge display—and single out whatever is relevant to the particular client.

Power stationery beefs up your image!

Your stationery may be the first and only thing many prospects see about you—so make your first impression a great one. Don't rely on computer generated business cards and stationery or items from the catalog at the local office supply store. They scream budget operation!

Instead, hire a top–notch graphics designer to prepare your letterhead, envelope, business cards and forms. And then have them printed by a good print shop. Everything will look and feel professional—and inspire confidence. This is especially important for home–based businesses, consultants and new start–ups.

Champagne results on beer budget: Coming up with basic ideas and rough layouts run up your bill. You can save a lot of time—and money—by helping the designer understand what you want. Collect stationery samples from other companies. Call local paper suppliers. Ask for paper sample kits from major paper mills. They often include award–winning letterheads, envelopes, business cards and other useful items. Armed with these, show the designer your preferences.

Changes and special demands will kill you. Carefully check all text and rough designs before type is set and art produced. If you can't afford a professional designer, have a good quick printer or desktop publisher prepare stationery based on your samples. Forms preprinted with graphics and multicolored designs are another economy option (see section elsewhere). But remember, don't cut corners here. Stationery is a big but onetime expense. Done right, it will produce continuous dividends for you.

Sound big, too!

Don't forget your telephone image. Answering machines and call waiting strongly suggest small–time operation! Invest in voice mail and other high–tech telephone services. Or hire an answering service—in addition to having a human being answer your phone, many will accept mail and provide other basic services. See the telephone sales chapter for complete details and more tips.

15

Retail tactics and strategies for success

How to fight Mammoth Mart!

Explaining how could take a whole new book. But here's a few basic ways to increase your sales even when you have to fight huge retailers: They need big volume to survive—so go the opposite direction. Localize. Find out everything you can about local tastes and act accordingly. Stock merchandise with area school logos, local attractions and one of a kind items Mammoth Mart will never even notice.

Focus on giving each customer highly personal service. Build their loyalty by being the person who always finds exactly what they need or want. This means you have to ask lots of questions, keep notes—and call them when you have what they want (see next tip).

Know your merchandise. Be able to tell the customer exactly why your goods are a better value and cheaper in the long run. Finally, provide the kind of assistance major stores simply cannot offer. Big stores hand you the item and a manual—be different, walk the buyer through a complete demonstration. Urge them to call you anytime they have a question. If necessary, make house calls to help the buyer. Remember, many people still can't program their own VCRs—offering a great sales opportunity for the service–oriented business.

Know your customers—and call

Business to business sellers often keep detailed records of their customers' needs and preferences— and call them when they see something the customer might want. Do the same. Keep records for sizes, color preferences and other basics. If you see something they might like, call.

Similarly, if a customer asks or calls about something they want but can't find, offer to locate it. Take their name and phone number—and go hunting. Even if you don't find the item, you'll have a name for your mailing list and someone you can call for future goods.

Give windows proper attention

Window displays are one of few sales tools that have the rare power to create impulse buying—and immediate sales results. Even so, window displays don't receive much attention. It's probably because a good window display looks like more work than it really is. Here are 10 tips for great windows with minimal effort:

1. Work within available space. A common mistake is cramming too much in a window. Don't try to show everything you sell. Spread things apart and display large items—so window contents are easily viewed from afar. But don't make it too empty, either.

2. Sell what you stock. Another common mistake is displaying what's not available inside. This practice infuriates many shoppers. Why make enemies? Display one of a kind clearance or sale items but mark them with small signs explaining what they are. Use signs like "Special price—last one!"

3. Avoid "permanent" sales. Promote sales and other special events with large, eye–catching signs. But remove your sale signs when the event ends. Otherwise, you undermine your credibility. People who pass by frequently will notice your seemingly endless sale and react accordingly—they won't believe you when it's the real thing.

4. Build around a theme. Base it on a season, sport, event, product, etc. A theme unifies everything. It saves you work selecting display items and signs.

5. Bright light is right. Use strong lighting so people can see what you sell. Add extra lights to brighten up otherwise dark and forgotten corners.

6. Use light, motion tricks. Things that flash and move grab the eye. Attract attention with strings of multiple blinking Christmas lights, a single large flashing or revolving light. Include animated, motorized displays. Try a videoplayer showing tapes of your wares.

Set up a toy train pulling car loads of your product. Create eye–arresting two–sided mobiles with bold, bright posters. Staple them back to back and add colorful or foil streamers. Use a small fan to keep everything turning and moving slowly.

7. Add real life. Few people can pass a window full of kittens or puppies without stopping. That's the pulling power of real life. Incorporate life with live product demonstrations. Draw attention with a midday fashion show, a handcrafter, an author signing books . . . whatever suits your business.

8. Swap display props. Window display props can be expensive. To cut costs, trade display items with other merchants. You can also rent props at theatrical supply stores and from window display companies. Check your suppliers for display resources.

9. Change something small every day. This will grab the attention of regular passers–by. Simplify your work with a feature of the day sign or a flexible display area. Get a changeable letter sign or a small electronic message board.

Even a small chalkboard will do if you use colorful chalks and are deft at lettering. Remember, people passing by could be customers now . . . if your window entices them to enter.

10. Above all, keep windows fresh, clean! Dead flies and sun faded, water–stained warped signs cost you money. Clean your windows inside and outside weekly. And redo the entire window display at least once a month.

Bundle to raise average sales size

You probably try to sell accessories and related products or services whenever you close a major sale. It's a lot easier if you bundle these extras together as a single–price package. As an added enticement, feature a special package price tied to purchasing the original item.

Car companies have successfully sold comfort, convenience and appearance protection packages for years. And many consumer products are offered in bundles. Bundling also is an alternative to price cuts. If a key product or service isn't selling well, add a premium of lesser value to it. Then sell the combination at the original price. You avoid a price cut and might increase sales enough to cover the premium's cost.

Use in–house promotions aggressively

Surprising numbers of customers—including regulars—are unaware of all the services or products a business offers. Or they may not associate that item with you. Remedy? If you are a store, stick flyers in every customer's bag. Promote new items, services—and other things they may not know about.

Use signs or flyers to promote upcoming seasons, specials. Many hotels, for example, run Christmas in July promotions at their restaurants. They remind managers and others who dine there to book Christmas functions early while the best dates are available. Restaurants can also use their placemats to push new menu items and banquet space. And you can always conduct joint in–house promotions with noncompetitive businesses.

Sell hard at the point of purchase

Point–of–purchase (POP) displays, posters and signs are essential to increase sales to customers already in your establishment. POP items can trigger impulse buying—and encourage people to purchase more than they intended.

Give them reasons to buy. Use plenty of bright colored signs and "shelf talkers" to promote sales, special merchandise, deals and products or services they may not know you offer. Turn on the emotions with big, beautiful, colorful posters and displays. Place posters and displays where customers have to see them, especially near the items being sold. Display them on walls, shelves and in offbeat places like bathrooms, dressing rooms, waiting areas and lobbies.

Check suppliers for free POP supplies. If they can't help, make your own displays, signs and posters. Or cut a barter deal with a local graphics design house. You spent a bundle bringing in customers—now turn them into sales with a strong point of–purchase effort.

Spark sales with 'how–to' aids

Do–it–yourself stores and services should give customers how–to videotapes and guides at cost or free. Don't just display them in a rack—aggressively offer them to do–it–yourselfers. You'll build loyalty, generate word–of–mouth advertising and increase sales. The reason is customers who successfully complete projects are more likely to try new ones—with supplies from you.

Zap offensive phrases

"You have to" and "you need to" may sound familiar. Well meaning retail and counter employees often utter these phrases in complaint situations. Unfortunately, most people interpret them as stone–walling or a kiss off. Many also find these lines patronizing.

Meanwhile the upset customer is thinking "I'm doing you a favor. I can take my business a lot of other places. I don't 'have to' or 'need to' do anything!" Banish those verbal firebombs. Train employees to use conciliatory terms. Above all, an immediate "I'm sorry!" does wonders.

16

How to get free news publicity

Three steps for getting in the news

News stories about you and your business in newspapers, magazines, on radio and TV can produce sales—at a fraction of the cost of advertising. You also gain credibility and respect. Here are three basic steps for creating news publicity:

1. Find a story idea

Media people want things that will interest their audiences. That includes many seemingly common occurrences because they are positive, upbeat and somehow out–of–the–ordinary. Good story subjects include:

Anything new! A new store, building, look, branch, division, service, product, franchise, process, machine, technique, technology, trend, project, employee, ownership—or when a new generation takes charge of the family business.

Achievements and milestones. Awards, commendations, prizes, recognition of any kind for you, employees, the business. Or the 1st, 10,000th, 1,000,000th or umpteenth anything. Also promotions, retirements, the anniversary of your business, service anniversaries, other personal marks. Attainment of major goals.

Seasonal tie–ins. Link yourself to the seasons, religious holidays, prominent birthdays and anniversaries, proclamation weeks and days established to commemorate causes.

Current events. Where applicable, offer the media background or comments on how a national issue, development or trend affects your community. Speak out on public concerns.

Human interest. Audiences and the media love stories that touch the heart. Personal profiles, success stories, handicaps overcome, people helping others and even hobbies or interests are good. Look at your employees on—and off—the job.

One–time happenings may be newsy. Consider overseas visitors inspecting a new process, big new contract, how you solved an old production problem. Anything that creates and saves jobs or helps the local economy is definitely news.

Find the "hook." Once you have your basic story idea, identify the single point that really stands out. That's the hook. Now bring your story idea to the media's attention.

2. Tell it to the media

Compile names of reporters, announcers, talk show hosts and others who cover stories like yours. Media directories are available at most libraries and chambers of commerce. Include addresses, telephone numbers and audience orientation.

Call or visit them. Sometimes a visit or call to your local media will get your story publicized, especially by smaller publications or broadcast stations. Just introduce yourself and ask who you should see about a story idea. But most media people will ask you to send them a news release. Don't panic — preparing one is easy. Here's how:

3. Prepare a short news release

A news release is simply facts about something given to the media in writing. You have to follow certain format rules but don't need to be a good writer since news people rewrite releases anyway. Rather it's more important to get in all the raw facts. Here's what you must include in your news release:

Source: Give your business name and address near the top of your sheet of paper so news people know who issued the release. You can use your normal business letterhead. **Contact:** Provide name and number of someone who can be reached for more information. Reporters often work odd hours so include a home number.

Release date: Again near top, list the phrase FOR IMMEDIATE RELEASE and date you sent out your release. This lets reporters know release can be used at will. **Headline:** Summarize your story's key point here. It quickly tells media what your story is all about.

Lead summary: Answer the critical questions of who, what, where, when, why and how in the first two paragraphs. **Supporting information:** The next paragraphs amplify your lead summary. List information in descending order of importance.

Look professional: Use standard letter–size paper on one side only. Always type your release, double space the story and leave one inch margins all around. Indent each paragraph and start the first with your city name. Never exceed two pages. If your release has two pages, type "more" at the bottom of page one. Indicate your story is finished by typing "end" after the last paragraph. Avoid fluff. Leave out advertising words like great, exciting and anything else that is self serving—otherwise your release will be discarded. Just provide all the facts. The media pros will do the rest.

When you think you are done, test your release. Read it aloud to another person—a bored individual who knows nothing about the release's contents. If they find it interesting and understandable, chances are the media will too. Print copies (never photocopy) of your release and distribute to the media. And hope for the best!

Should you make follow up calls? That depends. Most media people are very busy and don't have time for such calls. If the individual seemed particularly interested in your story, try calling four days after you sent the release but be very tactful.

Free radio, TV publicity—ask for it!

Making news isn't the only way to get free radio and TV publicity. You can also cash in by appearing on local radio and TV shows that feature guests. All you have to do is call them—and offer yourself as a guest. Here's how:

1. Look for a newsworthy or interesting angle in what you do. Shows want ratings so find something timely, exciting, seasonal, humorous, odd, educational, juicy, even titillating. Write down a short sales outline.

2. Call local stations. Ask for the talk show producer or host. For news and feature shows, request the assignment editor, news director or program director.

3. Ask to appear as a guest on your chosen topic. Immediately describe your news angle. They may ask you to send a proposal letter. Keep it under two pages. Sell the reason you should be on the show— especially why the audience would like your subject.

4. Think positive. Every business has a newsworthy angle. A lawncare specialist is a logical Spring guest. A pet shop owner can do a pre–Christmas show on selecting pets as gifts.

5. Let a friend call so you don't look like a publicity seeker. The friend can say, "You may want to know about so–and–so who can do an interesting show about . . . ." Remember, your likelihood of getting on shows depends on how newsworthy your story angle is.

Star on your own TV show!

You can reach thousands of prime prospects at very low cost—by starring on your own cable TV show. If you are an expert or leader in your field, contact local cable operators and special TV stations. Offer to host a "how–to" program.

A kitchen remodeler, for instance, can conduct clinics on kitchen redesign and remodeling. If the idea is really good, the station will try to sell ad time to appliance dealers and other appropriate suppliers. More than likely, they will ask you to buy the time—don't pass! It may be well worth the cost. Everyone who watches will be a real prospect.

Let's say 1,000 people who want their kitchens remodeled watch your show every week. What would it cost and how long would it take to reach that many solid prospects in another way? You can also make videotape copies and use them as an added sales tool or promotional giveaway.

'Niche' media: Ideal for small businesses

Niche media are specialty publications, cable channels, public radio stations and the like that cater to narrowly defined markets. They target a unique niche while mass media outlets attempt to be all things to all people.

They deserve special attention in your publicity and advertising efforts because (1) it's generally easier to obtain favorable free publicity from niche media and (2) they are often the best way to reach a special audience.

Big–time newspapers, radio and TV stations still command the largest audiences. But niche media are increasing steadily in quantity and quality, although they won't surpass the majors in overall influence anytime soon. Still, pursue them if you have a product or service that matches their audiences. Here are some niche media to investigate:

Newspapers: Start with shoppers, tabloids and other newspapers distributed free in your area. Check special interest newspapers aimed at religious, ethnic, fraternal, social, union, business, senior citizen and other groups. Such publications are often well read because their readers seek them out for information they cannot get elsewhere.

Radio: Look into college, high school and community public radio stations. Most don't accept ads but welcome show guests and run free announcements for community events.

Television: Again, check public stations. Many cable operators offer local access channels that have talk and educational shows. Try to get on them. Some schools, hospitals and military bases also operate closed circuit TV channels that may accept ads or trades.

Magazines and specialty publications: Choices abound here. Review club bulletins, company employee publications, church bulletins (see section elsewhere), singles newspapers, chamber of commerce publications, military installation newsletters, tourism guides, general business and city magazines.

The key to niche media success is two–fold. First, carefully analyze their audiences and editorial needs. Secondly, tailor your news release or your publicity idea to the medium's specific interests. Remember, they are trying to achieve financial success by meeting the needs and desires of a specific market—just like you.

Stunts and special events grab attention

Special events and stunts are activities you stage strictly to whip up interest and media publicity that will bring in prospects and profits. The more exciting or offbeat the idea, the more likely it is to succeed.

Holding an event shouldn't cost a lot if you do something

related to your business. A bicycle shop, for instance, can generate local publicity and traffic by offering free safety inspections. Similarly, a pet shop might offer pet care clinics.

The evening news often provides a timely opportunity for a bargain event. Along this line, a crime wave could be a good time for a security firm to announce free home security seminars. Linking yourself to a current cause, such as a disaster relief drive, is also productive.

Possible activities and themes are unlimited. You can stage contests, skill competitions, fundraisers, sidewalk sales, art and craft shows, flea markets, demonstrations, banquets, performances, award ceremonies, appreciation days, parties, debates, speeches, masquerade parties, carnivals, swaps, rallies and workshops to name a few possibilities. If you can't make an event work, let someone else stage an activity on your premises. Or consider an old–fashioned publicity stunt.

Publicity stunts are one–shot events done solely to create publicity. Attempts to be the biggest, best, worst or superlative of anything are common publicity stunts. In fact, many entries in *The Guinness Book of Records* are publicity stunts undertaken to break a record. They are less commonplace today but still work when done right.

Publicity events can be citywide. For example, Twinsburg, Ohio, which is America's only city named for twins, receives widespread publicity by holding an annual Twins Days Festival. The event celebrates sibling bonds and similarities. And celebrity look–alike contests always draw strong local attention. Other favorites are attempts to make the largest pizza or sandwich. Slices are then sold with proceeds given to charity.

Special events and stunts are quick attention getters. They are ideally suited to new businesses that can't afford advertising. But whether you are new or established, try to conduct at least two activities annually to keep your name in the news.

Piggyback on community events

Plan promotions, sales and activities that capitalize on upcoming local events. These can include conventions, athletic events, school activities, marathons and other citywide happenings. If the city is hosting a major track and field meet, for example, conduct a "make tracks to us" sale. Or offer your business as a collection point for Christmas donations for the needy and you may receive free media coverage.

Write for local newspapers

Local newspapers often accept useful and interesting "filler" stories. The reason is some smaller papers can't always find enough news on their own to fill their needs. This is especially true of stories with a local angle. You can help them—and get valuable free exposure for your business—by providing newsworthy information.

Start by contacting your local newspapers. Explain what you do. Offer to prepare—for free—a special feature or regular column with information interesting and useful to their readers. Ask them to include your name, business name, address and telephone number. But take what they give you!

You might end up a columnist and receive thousands of dollars in free exposure. If you do, reprint your articles and use them as sales tools that reinforce your credentials as an expert in your field.

Write letters to the editor

Writing a letter to the editor is a proven way to reach a large audience—for the price of a stamp or fax. For starters, virtually every newspaper has a letters page or column. Most newspapers, especially local publications, see themselves as their community's voice and record. For this reason, they welcome letters to the editor and guest editorial columns. Use letters to publicize upcoming events, developments in your field and add new information about a topic covered in a recent story—especially if it deals with your field and you were left out. You can also comment on local affairs or respond to unfair or erroneous attacks on your business or industry.

If you are refuting something negative about your company or industry, don't embarrass yourself. Make sure your letter is moderately toned, nonattacking and full of supporting facts.

Another approach is to have someone else write a letter for you. For example, thank you letters for community good deeds will help you win friends—and sales.

Become a national media source!

If you want exposure to media nationwide, consider a listing in the *Yearbook of Experts, Authorities & Spokespersons®*. Many reporters, news directors, talk show producers and others use this directory to find experts and guests. Listings start at $325. For more information, call Broadcast Interview Source at 202—333–4904. And before you know it, you'll be presented to thousands of media outlets as an authority or spokesperson in your field.

Free media information!

There are thousands of newspapers, magazines, specialty publications, newsletters, radio and TV stations out there—and it won't cost you a penny to find out which ones can help you reach your target customers. Just check out these valuable resources that are available at many public libraries:

Bacon's Publicity Checker. It lists 20,000 newspapers and magazines. *Broadcasting Yearbook* which includes all radio, TV and cable outlets in the U.S. and Canada. *Gale Directory of Publications.* It covers 25,000 newspapers, magazines and other publications by location. *Hudson's Newsletter Directory* which lists over 4,000 subscription newsletters by subject.

If you have national talk show potential, there's a directory just for you. It's *Talk Shows and Hosts on Radio.* This directory from Whitefoord Press of Dearborn, Michigan lists 1,052 radio talk shows and their hosts. It also provides biographical background on over 200 hosts as well as show format and topic information. Call 800—972–2584. Finally, some libraries carry locally prepared directories that often contain valuable hometown media information not listed in national directories. Be sure to ask about these.

Reprint favorable news stories

A favorable newspaper or magazine story is valuable because studies show people generally believe what they read, especially when they see it in the newspaper. But the story only helps you once—unless you reprint it. Then it works forever! Always reprint positive stories on white glossy paper stock for a class look. Then distribute the reprints like crazy.

Use reprints as ads, mailers

For added sales impact, turn your reprints into ads, posters and direct mail pieces. First, put a headline on the page. Say something like "Stop in for steaks that are the talk of the town." Then use the story itself as a graphic. Finally, add the name of your business, address, hours and other information at the bottom. You can enlarge it as a poster or reduce it for use as a mailer.

17

PR: Do good by doing good

The truth about public relations

Public relations is everything you do other than paid advertising to make people aware of your business in a favorable light. It's all about making friends and allies. You make community contacts you may need someday (such as when you have a permit or license problem). And you meet people who can give you business or refer business to you.

Don't expect miracles because you rarely profit directly from public relations. Rather, it creates a friendly atmosphere—and opens doors for making money. That's why charitable giving and other forms of community involvement can be politically prudent and pay for itself many times over. The key is to find the right causes.

How to find causes that help you

It's financially impossible to help every worthwhile cause. The trick is to find those that also benefit your business. Ask these questions when you consider a community activity:

1. Will you make useful contacts with politicians, government officials, civil leaders, neighbors, activists and other community elements who can help or hurt your business?

2. Will you meet prime new prospects or others who can direct business your way?

3. Is the sponsoring organization willing to associate your name with the undertaking and to what degree?

4. Will the activity produce favorable publicity for you and your business?

5. Are you likely to cover your out–of–pocket expenses?

The extent you can answer yes to these questions suggests how beneficial your participation is likely to be. Whatever you do, keep your eye on the bottom line.

Toot your horn when you help

Tell the world whenever you perform a good deed. If you don't, chances are nobody else will. Find tasteful—but clear ways—to advise customers, prospects, politicians and anyone else who affects your business.

The battle is largely won if you get your name associated with the charitable endeavor from the start. But that may not have happened. And you should not assume key people will see it in the news. Instead cover your bets with these tips:

Ask the charitable organization for a congratulatory letter. Send copies with your mailings. Use reprints of favorable news stories the same way.

Try to get the beneficiary of your concern to give you a plaque or award which they announce to the media. Take anything, no matter how seemingly insignificant—everything adds up and enhances your credibility and reputation.

Finally, don't let self–promotion scare you. If your charitable acts are genuine and beneficial, people will be glad to know they are dealing with a business that supports the community.

Pay with product cost dollars

Hide your cash when asked to support a charitable undertaking. Instead, use product dollars. A restaurant, for instance, should offer to trade a $100 gift certificate for a $100 school ad—and suggest the school use the certificate as a door prize. The restaurant's real cost is far less than a $100. Yet the restaurant receives the ad plus publicity from the drawing.

Creative giving conserves cash!

You can also avoid paying with cash by contributing products, services or equipment as described in the next several tips. For example, you might contribute some kind of coupon. A restaurant could donate $1.00 meal discount coupons to a Scout troup who would sell them door–to–door to raise funds. The restaurant receives a free plug whenever a Scout addresses a potential customer. Additionally, the restaurant should pick up new business if the distribution area is carefully targeted. Another good approach is to call local charities and work out coupon trades in advance.

Offer a community dollars program

You can help local charitable groups—and increase your sales—with a community dollars program. Instruct legitimate charity groups to register with you. Organization members then save all their cash register tapes for a specified time, such as four months. The group turns the tapes over to you, usually monthly, and receives a 1% or 2% rebate on the total tapes turned in. The rebate can be in cash or for goods and services from your business.The more they shop at your business, the more they earn—while your sales rise accordingly.

As for paperwork, prepare a one–page application form. Request basics such as organization name, leader, phone number, address, number of members and nature of their charitable work. But also require them to describe exactly how they will use the rebate money. Finally, add a paragraph in which they swear the organization is a bona fide nonprofit organization while you retain the right to cancel the program any time. Lastly, have the group representative sign the form.

Lend your way to publicity and sales

Many times publicity or tie–in opportunities come your way but you don't have the bucks to participate. Consider lending out your product, services or equipment. Surely you have something sitting idle for awhile that you can spare—in trade for getting your name and sales slogan on every ticket, sign or ad used for the event you are assisting.

Donate excess to charity

Donating excess product or capacity to worthwhile causes costs little but returns goodwill and free publicity. This is a natural for bakers, caterers, stores and others dealing in perishables and businesses with regular excess capacity.

Many theaters, health clubs, beauty shops and hotels have predictable slow periods. Use the excess capacity to advantage by offering it to people who would not or could not otherwise use your services.

Give slow selling and surplus items

Cut your losses on poor selling goods, surplus and outdated supplies by donating them to worthwhile causes. Aside from doing good, you will also reap goodwill and free publicity. Also check into the tax write–off benefits.Just about any item in good condition is valuable to someone. This includes hard–to–sell merchandise, irregulars, surplus supplies, outdated promotional goodies and technologically obsolete office equipment. Take a hard, realistic look at your business attic and turn some of that trash into treasure.

Provide community service space

If you have good visibility and traffic, invite local Scouts and others to post event signs in your business. Also provide space for a fund–raising booth or display.

You'll build goodwill and contacts that you can capitalize on when you want to distribute coupons and conduct other promotional activities described elsewhere in this book. You can also trade the space for free ads in their publications. Or you can ask them to distribute your sales material to their members and provide other services for you.

Trade meeting space for publicity

Community groups, clubs and organizations always need places to meet. If you have the room, offer them meeting space in exchange for a free ad or story in their publications. They can also distribute coupons and sales material to their members. You'll receive free publicity, make useful contacts, generate goodwill and expose your business to potential new customers who have never been there. If you don't have space, see what else you can trade.

Form community advisory panel

Form a community advisory board if community actions or public opinion affect your business. A board could help improve communications between you and the community. For example, it's a good way to identify potential problems and issues that could hurt you. And it's another way to explain how your firm's health affects the community.

Some tips: Recruit elected officials, religious leaders, celebrities and officers from civic, fraternal and social groups. Always be open, honest. Permit debate. Include friends and past critics. Find ways to adopt some of their suggestions. And socialize! Use meetings to build bridges and create new allies.

Free tours yield publicity, sales

Schools, churches, youth organizations, senior programs, bus tour operators and others are always looking for field trip ideas. If your business is even remotely interesting, call them and offer your place as a destination.

To cash in, give adults discount coupons, sales literature and samples. Give kids goodie bags with coupons and samples to take home to parents. Tell local media tours are available so they can advise their audiences and readers. And definitely call the media when a group is coming—they may cover the actual trip. After a tour, ask the sponsoring organization for a thank you letter. Use your testimonials in ads and displays. Bottom line? Tours can be used for publicity, to create sales, build community ties and recruit future employees.

Invite Bloodmobile for media mentions

Bloodmobiles and blood drives often receive free location announcements from local media. If your business can host a blood drive, call the Red Cross and offer your facilities. The media may mention your business in numerous public service announcements during the week prior to the visit. Another approach is to offer your business as a drop–off center for programs collecting food, clothes or other items for charity. Working with high visibility disaster relief drives is also very effective.

18

Ways you can afford mass media

Eight rules for maximizing results

Don't automatically dismiss mass media advertising as too expensive. Rates tend to be high but only because big newspapers, major magazines, radio and TV stations reach huge audiences and can deliver impressive results fast. There are ways to cut costs—and even get free ads—when you need their audience numbers and impact. If you are considering mass media, here are some points to keep in mind:

1. Prepare carefully. No promotional vehicle can guarantee results—but large mass media expenditures leave you far less room for problems and errors.

2. Identify prime prospects before you proceed. Prepare a precise profile of your target customer using this book's market research tips. As always, the objective is to identify the fewest people who can do you the most good.

3. Let customers help pick media. Ask your current customers about their favorite newspapers, magazines, radio and TV shows. Armed with this information, contact media sales representatives for advertising rates.

4. Buy only what you want! Advertise only where the audience consists mainly of prime prospects. Don't be sold only by cost per thousand (cpm) figures that indicate this or that is a bargain for you—always determine how many of those people are prospects. You want quality not quantity.

5. Negotiate ad rates. Media rates are negotiable. Some prime newspaper positions or broadcast shows may be untouchable. But all else is usually open to discussion. When you negotiate, start super low.

6. Always monitor results. Use a special telephone number, a coupon, premium—anything—that will show whether the ad was worth your outlay. If you can't do this, don't advertise!

Free and subsidized co–op ads

Co–op advertising is an arrangement in which suppliers pay up to 100% for ads placed on your behalf. You agree to sell and promote their products or services. In turn, they pay for ads to help you sell their products or services. It's that simple.

Some suppliers will pick up the entire advertising expense while others will pay a percentage. Many will partially reimburse you if you include their names in your ads. You can cut your ad costs sharply by listing several suppliers in your ads.

To get started, ask your supplier reps about their co–op programs. Also ask your newspaper rep for help since many papers have a co-op ad specialist. Finally, check with trade associations and other who may offer co–op programs.

Organize advertising co–op

If your suppliers don't offer co–op advertising, join forces with other businesses to share mass media costs. Retail merchants have done this for years but the concept can also work for service providers, professionals and even businesses that sell to other businesses. You can team up on the basis of location, product and service.

Remnant ad space big bargain!

Unsold newspaper and magazine ad space or TV and radio time can't be stored for sale at a later date. Consequently, you can often find great media buys—if you are ready to act fast. The trick is to ask your media sales representative when they stop taking ads for a particular day or edition. And then call a few days before their deadline and offer to participate at a drastically discounted rate. Shoot for 60 to 80% off the normal rate. Or ask them to call you when they have remnant space. You may have to wait awhile but the savings will be worth it.

They may take you up on your offer as a last resort to salvage some revenue from otherwise wasted ad space or time. To capitalize, you must have your ad prepared and ready to go.

Two–step ads save and sell!

You can wage a widespread advertising campaign on a tiny budget through the two–step advertising process.

First place brief classified ads in various publications or under several headings. You can also mail cheap postcards.

You include only enough information to whet the readers' appetite to write for more details. This technique eliminates the need for expensive display ads. You also avoid telephone handling problems and costs. And since readers must take action to get more information, you qualify your list by weeding out many nonproductive lookers.

In step two, answer inquiries with sales literature, personalized letters or phone calls and personal visits. People who place orders go on a prime mailing list and receive regular mailings. For maximum results, make a mailing to your respondents six weeks after your initial ad campaign. Conduct repeat mailings every four to six weeks as long as the orders generated cover your costs.

Flag main ad with classifieds

Run brief classified ads that direct readers to your main ad in the same publication. You'll get a larger, broader audience for modest additional cost. Place ads under appropriate listings and you'll reach potential customers who may miss your main ad. The reason is some people don't read or even browse through the entire publication but they do read classifieds—especially when they are looking for a specific thing.

Pay only for results!

Paying only for actual advertising results is a great deal if you can get it. Some newspapers and broadcasters may be willing to do just that through per–order or per–inquiry agreements.

You agree in advance how much you will pay them for every order or inquiry your ad generates—and pay only for results. You don't have any up–front expenses either. Needless to say, the radio, TV or newspaper outlet is taking a big chance and will want a large piece of the action to get involved.

An effective way to track orders and inquiries is also essential. Advertisers have successfully sold many different products and services with this approach, especially on late night or weekend radio and TV.

Newspaper inserts affordable

It costs only pennies per piece to insert and deliver sales material in local newspapers. Consequently, inserts can be cheaper than large display ads, even after allowing for printing expenses. You can best use inserts to reach prospects in a specific geographic area. They are a good alternative when direct mail can't or is too expensive. On the down side, some sources contend readers don't see half of all newspaper inserts! If you try inserts, add a coupon to track results.

Syndicated radio: Low–cost national reach

A small business with an 800 number can sell for less nationwide by advertising on syndicated radio. Many radio stations save money by using syndicated programs they often receive for free. The syndicators make money by selling ad space. You benefit by reaching a larger audience for less than it usually costs to buy many radio stations separately. You also retain control over who hears your ad. Check media directories (see tip elsewhere for names) at your local library to get syndicator names or call local radio stations.

Become radio station premium

"The tenth caller will receive a free tune up at . . . ." Sound familiar? Publicity seeking businesses furnish most radio station prizes. To cash in, call the advertising or promotions director at local radio stations. Offer your products or services as prizes in trade for an ample plug. But don't pay for the prizes! Persuade your suppliers to donate the prizes you give radio stations. Tell them *they* are the ultimate winners from your publicity efforts. You can also barter your stuff for regular commercial time.

Save 15% on display advertising

You can save 15% on what you pay to run display ads by forming your own in–house advertising agency. It's easy and perfectly honest. The price you pay for newspaper or magazine ad space is usually structured to give a 15% commission to recognized ad agencies. If you prepare and place your own ads, the newspaper keeps the 15%—unless you have your own ad agency to collect the 15% commission for you.

The key is to establish your own in–house adverting agency that looks like a separate, independent business. It takes a little work. But if you place a lot of display ads, the savings could be substantial. Here's how to do it:

1. Start an agency. Give it a name that has no connection to your main business.

2. Use a different address than your business address. A separate Post Office box usually suffices.

3. Give the agency a separate identity. Print inexpensive stationery and envelopes. Above all, prepare an Ad Insertion Order Form. Get one from a friend, the library or your newspaper ad rep and adapt it to your new agency.

4. Open a separate checking account in the new agency's name—pay all ad bills from this account. Put your spouse or someone else's name on it and have them sign checks. Ditto for the Ad Insertion Order Form.

5. Place all ads and conduct related business through your new in–house ad agency.

19

How to use print, radio, TV effectively

What newspapers do best

Big newspapers offer you several advantages, among them: **Immediacy.** Three out of four consumers reportedly turn to them for purchasing information. **Credibility.** The overall news content adds a factual air to your advertising. **Depth.** Newspapers give you room to describe your offering in detail. **Flexibility.** You can change ads easily and submit them on a few days' notice. **Reach.** Actual readership usually exceeds circulation. Industry experts claim 2.7 readers see each copy of a newspaper. **Durability.** Prospects can save your ad and refer back to it when ready to buy.

Success secrets: A powerful headline is critical. Studies show four out of five readers don't go past headlines. And those with a benefit sell more than those that don't. A winning headline directly addresses your prime prospects, includes your basic message—and a solid benefit or reason to buy from you. Illustrations are the next best way to snare readers. Actual photographs outpull drawings.

Always use simple layouts. Keep ads organized, easy to follow. Use white space to encourage, aid reading. If you include a photograph, place a caption under it—they are read twice as much as regular body copy. And be complete. Give readers everything they need to know. Don't forget your address, telephone number, hours and other basics. When placing your ad, request a position above the page middle. If you run a small ad frequently, always place it on the same page so target prospects will become familiar with it.

Magazines have special strengths

Don't lump magazines with newspapers. They do share some strengths, such as suitability for long ad copy. But unlike newspapers, **magazines provide pinpoint audience selectivity.** Name a target market and you'll find a magazine tailored to it.

Other distinct pluses: Long life. Magazines are read repeatedly, passed to others—and can produce results long after published.

There's also involvement. Magazines are closely read, considered. Readers treat ads similarly. Many identify with their favorite magazines so you gain credibility by association. Additionally, magazines are ideal for projecting a quality image since many use better paper and premium printing.

Secrets for success: Consider magazine ads when you want to (1) reach an audience that extends beyond your locality and (2) increase consumer confidence in a product or service. For hometown impact only—at a reasonable price—advertise in a major magazine's local or regional edition.

Another trick is to run a single ad in a prestigious local edition. Reprint the ad with the line "as seen in Big Shot Magazine" and give out reprints forever.

If money is real tight, run a classified ad using the two–step technique described elsewhere. Finally, observe the design and content tips discussed in the newspaper section.

Radio targets with precision

Radio's big strength is selectivity. Intense competition has forced many stations to serve sharply defined market segments. So you can reach prime prospects with extreme precision and economy. **Other advantages: Ubiquity.** America has over 400 million radios in homes, cars, offices, factories, stores, on beaches . . . everywhere. Radio also is fast, flexible. You can exploit current events with on–air announcements—best of all, ads delivered live cost nothing to produce.

You can intrude. The right sounds demand attention even when listeners are doing something else. You can also **personalize** and "talk" one–on–one with your prospects. Use their code words, language, music to gain attention, build trust, motivate action.

Success secrets: Radio ads pass in a flash, vanish in thin air. Prospects can't go back and reread them. Simplicity is critical. Messages must be obvious, direct and limited to one basic theme. Open fast! Lead with your biggest benefit and name—before listeners can switch stations.

Commercials initially are missed or barely absorbed. Some say four exposures pass before a message sticks in a listener's head. Repeat and concentrate. Air ads only a couple days a week on specific programs and stations. If funds are short, don't reduce frequency. Cut back instead on the number of programs and stations. Try to hit a target audience with at least 10 spots a day. To stretch money, run ads in a cycle of one week on, one week off.

Ask air personalities to deliver your spots live. Many have large, loyal followings. If air personalities like your offering, they'll sell it better than you. Let air personalities work from a fact sheet rather than a script. Your ad will be different each time it is delivered—and you'll avoid the repetition that comes from a prerecorded ad.

Lastly, shop around. Many radio stations target the same market segments. With the strong competition, you might find attractive deals. Negotiate the number of spots, not the dollar amount of your buy. Go in knowing exactly who will give you the most spots at times you want for your fixed budget.

TV still packs 'em in!

No other media matches TV's power to sell your product with sight, sound and motion. What's more, nearly every home has a TV—which the average family watches over six hours each day. No wonder more Americans rely on the tube for entertainment and information than any other medium. To cash in, however, you had to buy a bigger audience than you needed. This put TV advertising beyond the means of most small businesses. But no longer.

Success secrets: TV is splintering like radio did. There are hundreds of shows and stations that deliver precise audiences—at very low ad rates. Like radio, frequency is desirable. But a single cheap 30–second spot weekly on a special interest program could pay off handsomely. Remember, you are reaching real prospects. Also check cable operators for geographic packages tailored your trade area.

As for commercials, **the picture must tell your story.** Words reinforce the visual, not the reverse. Exploit TV's visual power—demonstrate your goods. Testimonials also work if participants look, sound natural. Avoid gimmicks, props. Instead, portray people. And start fast. Plug your best benefit and name in the opening seconds or you'll lose viewers. Keep it simple—sell one big idea and keep reinforcing it. Producing commercials is expensive. To cut costs, have the TV studio or cable company produce yours. A well–planned simple commercial can be done for under $1,000.

20

Steps for sales material that really sells

Put it on paper to sell!

Like it or not, you probably need some kind of sales literature. The simple reality is most people want something tangible to review when considering a purchase, especially for higher–priced items. There are several psychological reasons for this:

1. "Feelability" is credibility. The printed piece represents documentation—it is proof you are an established, serious business. Printed literature implies roots, experience, stability, professionalism. In short, credibility.

You can control your "credibility picture" by the appearance, content, tone and style of your printed material. For instance, a lavish four–color brochure on expensive paper makes a direct mail operation run from a kitchen table look like a multi–million dollar corporation.

2. It reminds, resells. Your printed sales piece keeps selling long after the sales call or encounter. It keeps your sales message alive in the prospect's mind. But it also sells everyone else who sees it, creating new sales opportunities.

3. It closes. Many prospects just need a little more reassurance that they are making the right decision. Your sales literature could provide the extra incentive needed. Others need or want additional information to make a final buying decision. A sales piece is absolutely essential in these situations—and gives you a distinct advantage over competitors who don't have printed sales material.

Basic flyer has million uses!

As vital as it is, your sales material doesn't have to be costly. The cheapest approach is to arm yourself with a generous supply of flyers—they cost just pennies to produce but have countless valuable applications.

Flyers are usually 8 1⁄2 x 11 inches printed one color on one side. But variations abound. Some businesses print a half sheet flyer to save money. Others prefer a 4 x 9 inch piece that fits regular business envelopes and standard display racks. The small 4 x 9 size is also handy for crowded counters and doubles as a mailing stuffer or insert. Here's how to get the most from a flyer:

1. Make it versatile. List all the places and ways you might use it. Prepare a generalized flyer to fill all the needs. If you can't, don't worry—print several versions since flyers cost as little as three or four cents each in quantities of a thousand.

2. Include basics. Capture the reader's attention with a headline that screams out the most important benefit from dealing with your business. Raise awareness—and the desire to buy—by listing all your benefits and features in the flyer.

3. Be complete. Cover everything the buyer needs to make a buying decision. This includes your full address, directions for getting there, telephone and fax numbers (with area code), credit cards accepted, check policy and hours of operation.

4. Keep it current. Flyers are inexpensive and easy to reprint quickly. So keep yours updated—don't hurt your sales by giving customers old, erroneous or incomplete information.

Use flyers to supplement catalogs, brochures and other more expensive and less flexible literature.

5. Think big! Use bright paper stock and a color ink for stronger visual impact. Add pictures, graphics. And for sales impact, distribute flyers widely through the 50 locations listed elsewhere in this book.

Good sales hook snares minds

A good hook is the key to effective sales literature—and all promotional activities. It's the brief message people remember long after they've forgotten where they saw or read it. You add it to everything from business cards to stationery, vehicles, sales literature and advertisements.

The effective hook summarizes the big benefit prospects get from your product or service. It is also believable and catchy.

Consider Greyhound Bus Company's timeless ". . . and leave the driving to us!" Or "Don't leave home without it!" from American Express, Miller Lite Beer's "tastes great, less filling" and the tourism slogan "I love New York!"

Developing a slogan costs little or nothing, just mental exertion. Once you develop a good one, stay with it because your catchy phrase needs time to get around. But once it does, your hook will endure and keep selling!

Carry on a personal conversation

Most people love to talk but suddenly go blank when they have to write something—or else the written words come out stiff and formal. To get around this common problem, make your sales communications sound as if you are carrying on a conversation with one person. Use "you" and "your" liberally to achieve this. Make each potential customer feel special even though you are communicating to a wide audience.

Power words that increase sales

Words are one of the most powerful free sales weapons. The right words in a headline will persuade prospects you have what they want—and ignite the impulse to buy. Yet the right words cost no more than the wrong ones.

Listed below are 62 words used frequently in successful sales material. You may not find the exact power word you need for your headline or sales piece. But you can still use them to jump start your imagination—and sales:

announcing	attention	bargain	bonus
check	compare	complete	confidential
discover	earn	easy	end
exciting	exclusive	facts	free
fun	gain	gift	good
guarantee	helpful	here	how–to
hurry	important	improved	informative
interesting	introducing	learn	love
look	money	new	now
offer	personal	popular	profit
proven	quick	rebate	refundable
reliable	results	safe	sale
save	sex	special	stop
success	tested	today	try
urgent	wanted	win	yes
you	yours		

Incorporate the above words wherever possible in your headlines and body text. Apply the word as is or try a variation. For instance, guarantee can be used as "guaranteed."

Don't offend in sales material

You can accidently lose customers by using words and images that seem fine to you—but are offensive to some groups. Check your sales material from a prospect's viewpoint and eliminate possible problems.

Replace gender specific words with generic terms. Don't employ "he" or "man" to stand for both women and men. Use "people" or "person" and "their." Reword phrases like "for men who care" to "people who care." A product or service intended only for men or women is an obvious exception. Similarly, "salesmen" suffices when the salesperson indeed is a man. If in doubt, go generic.

Be equally on guard for racial, religious and other stereotypes. Avoid outdated images and approaches. For instance, if you haven't already, retire that sales brochure showing a bikini–clad model demonstrating your deluxe plastic molding machine. The same applies to offensive calendars and tasteless ad specialties that somehow persist in an era when women are a major market force. Remember the golden rule of good taste: When in doubt, don't!

Proofread for professional look

You can't afford to look like an amateur when you're competing with bigger, established competitors— and nothing makes you look more amateurish than a sales brochure or ad full of spelling and grammatical errors.

It just takes one glaring headline error, for example, to undercut the credibility of an otherwise convincing sales brochure. If you prepare your own sales literature, find someone else to proofread your material for you. Don't rely on spell checkers and computer aids—they can't distinguish between drunk "drivers" and "divers."

Don't trust professional typesetters and ad agencies either. They're usually pretty good but they are human. If you use them, try to double check everything yourself, especially headlines. Good proofreading isn't exactly a sales tip but will help you present a professional image that complements your sales activities.

Personalize sales presentations

Most people know a form sales piece when they see it—especially the slick, glossy four–color documents that scream hard sell. So flatter your friends: Send them a personalized letter or even a hand–written note. Tailor it to the recipient. Work in a shared personal anecdote or two. Customize the presentation to the person's company, needs and objectives.

Free and low–cost sales graphics

Good pictures and art are big factors in the cost of preparing effective sales material, whether done in–house or outside. To save money, use free or low–cost public domain and stock photographs, illustrations, clip art and other graphics. Common sources are your suppliers, trade associations, business development agencies and other promotion–minded organizations. Simple clip art of all kinds is sold in book form at art supply and book stores.

Clip art ranging from basic to highly sophisticated is also available on computer disks from computer mail order companies. Additional resources include excellent retail ad templates, seasonal illustrations and art in various styles. Check computer magazines for supplier ads.

Custom photography can be quite expensive. If you just need a general photo, buy a stock picture from a stock photograph supplier. See Photography—Stock Photos in your Yellow Pages. Or check out the low–cost public domain photographs found at some public libraries.

While at the library, take a look the *Literary Market Place.* This directory for the book and publishing industry contains a list of stock photo agencies.

21

Dirt cheap do–it–yourself market research

Shoe leather research free!

Good market research is the foundation of everything you do. But if you can't afford professional research help, conduct your own shoe leather market research. You'll gather important information at the grassroots level. Yet it won't cost you a cent except for your time and some shoe leather.

Schedule regular visits to your competition. Then pound the pavement. Observe their location, facilities, operations, service, goods, clientele, other basics. Where you can, talk to customers. Stop 'em in the parking lot, on the street, wherever. Ask why they are there—rather than at your place.

Ingenuity is required but it can be done. For instance, a mall parking lot conversation might start like this: "Excuse me, I'm new here and I've never tried Jones Hardware before. How are they? And what about X hardware (your store) . . . are they any good?" Patience and the right questions could yield valuable research that even professional researchers can't develop.

Many astute business people have solved otherwise puzzling sales riddles by merely observing competitors' operations or conversing with their patrons. It's also an affordable way to stay in touch with real people—and potential customers.

Stick pins—cheap, good geographic research

Every business must know the geographic area from which it draws most of its customers. This is essential to target promotional efforts accurately—and to avoid situations in which you give coupons or other special deals to existing customers while trying to reach new prospects. A cheap and easy way to determine your main geographic or trade area is stick pin research.

Simply use color stick pins or press apply dots to show on a map where your customers are located. Get addresses from your current customers or records. Then use different colors to show the exact location of various types of customers (large, small, active, etc.). Stick pin research isn't very fancy but you'll get nearly the same results as professional research costing much more.

Candy bowl—trite research that works

Having people put their business cards in a candy bowl to win prizes is hopelessly trite. But it can yield a goldmine of useful information for walk–in businesses. Start with a candy bowl, briefcase or some other receptacle. Then give people a chance to win prizes by depositing their business cards. Provide blank cards for people who don't have business cards. The prize is irrelevant—just make it good enough to get people to participate. Now the critical part!

Go through the cards on a regular basis. Some businesses, for example, may want to check them daily or even several times a day. The cards are a good way to determine who your customers are, where they live or work, what they do or when they come in. It's also a great way to gather names for mailing lists, telemarketing campaigns and joint promotions (see tips elsewhere).

Simple surveys generate sales leads

Try including a brief survey form or card with your sales literature and mailings. The reason is recipients who take time to respond often are good sales prospects—even if they don't have an immediate need for your goods or services. Typical questions could include: Does our product meet your needs? What do you need that we don't offer? What can we do better? May we contact you for additional information?

You can use the survey as a direct sales tool by including a sample of your product with the survey—ask recipients to comment on the sample. Or offer them a sample of your goods or services as a reward for completing the survey.

Let competitors improve your ads

You can improve your ads by systematically studying competitors' ad changes over an extended time. This is especially beneficial when you can't afford research and face larger, long–established competitors. The study also is an ideal project for a college marketing student. See elsewhere in this book for information about free help from local colleges.

First determine in which newspapers or magazines your competitors are likely to advertise. Then hit the local library and check ads for a two–year period. That's long enough for patterns to develop and to encompass seasonal variations.

Scrutinize everything! Note changes in publications used, ad placement within publications, headlines, body text, illustrations, ad style, language tone and size. Pay close attention to changes in specific headline words. A competitor may have found a word, phrase or headline that really sells—you will want to "borrow" what they learned at considerable expense. Also watch for coupons, bonus gifts, credit cards accepted, toll–free numbers, limited offers and other sales devices.

Note patterns. An ad that runs unchanged for a year or more is probably working. But changes suggest something was wrong or they found a better approach. Either way, you could save money and improve your sales results merely by monitoring the advertising practices of your competitors.

Keep monitoring rivals' ads

Once you have reviewed your competitors' old ads as described in the previous tip, don't stop! Build a scrapbook of all newspaper and magazine ads, flyers, brochures, coupons and anything else printed. Keep notes or tapes of radio and TV ads. Record dates, times, places, contents, media used. As before, the idea is to cash in on the market research efforts and expenditures of your bigger, better financed rivals.

Get on adversaries' mailing lists

This is an easy, effective and free way to keep track of what your competition is doing. If your name might be spotted, use the name of a friend or another family member. You might even buy something occasionally so you can sample their service and see how they handle active accounts.

Employ mystery shoppers

Mystery shoppers are a great way to find out how your competitors—and you—are performing. Have someone visit your key competitors on a regular schedule. Prepare a checklist for them.

Conversely, find someone your employees don't know to visit your business. You might want your mystery shopper to give your employees an on–the–spot reward, such as a $10 bill, for good service. You'll probably have to change shoppers after a couple of visits.

Actively solicit customer feedback

It's critical to know whether you are really satisfying your customers. Some businesses spend big bucks on consultants to learn how customers really feel. A cheaper alternative is to continuously solicit feedback yourself from your customers.

Don't say "How's everything?" and accept "Oh, everything's fine" as an answer. Too often things aren't fine. But most people are too timid to tell the truth or don't want to bother. Dig. Use openers like "What did you like best?" and "What can we do better?" Prepare a series of specific questions and ask them over and over. Change them as you identify problems so you're always checking into the right things.

Pump sales reps for information

It's human nature to be short with sales people who walk into your business cold. After all, they often disrupt your business and waste your time. Even so, be extra nice to them—they are in a position to help or hurt you. For starters, sales representatives can be a good source of information about your competitors since they probably call on them too. With a little tact and sugar, you can get sales leads, find out who's in trouble, new developments, etc. These sales reps may also talk to your clients and prospects—and the last thing you want is someone bad mouthing you all over town.

Listen to the grapevine

The California raisins had it right because you can learn a great deal about your business through the grapevine. Ask your regular customers, suppliers, sales reps and friends to tell you whenever they hear something about your company—no matter how unpleasant. And don't wait for them to call. Instead, solicit their comments when you call them.

Check license plates for customer names

Want the names of a competitor's customers? Have someone write down the license numbers of cars in the rival's parking lot for a week or so. Then get a state motor vehicle office or local police contact to convert the plate numbers to names and addresses for you. Send them discount coupons, sales literature and the like. Needless to say, check legalities first!

License plates yield location clues

Some states include a county of registration sticker on their license plates. If you live in such a state, this is a good way to gather location research information. In some states, certain license plate prefixes are sold from specific locations.

For example, plates starting with T might be sold at a center city agency while plates with B might be sold at a suburban outlet. You can usually get a list indicating which prefixes are sold where from your state motor vehicle department. This is an highly effective yet low–cost way to learn where potential customers live and work.

Personal checks—great data source

More and more people are including their telephone numbers as well as complete addresses on their personal checks. If you want to build up a great direct mail and telemarketing list, be sure to copy this information from checks before you deposit them. Even if you don't need the information, you may be able to sell or rent the list to someone else. First check local banking and privacy regulations.

22

Where to find free marketing help

Tap SCORE for free business advice

You can get professional business counseling and training—free—from experienced business people by calling SCORE. That's the Service Corps of Retired Executives. The organization's counselors provide free information and advice for virtually every type of business. Best of all, a SCORE counselor or team will help you assess and define problems.

To reach SCORE, check your local phone book under SCORE, the Small Business Administration or call your local chamber of commerce. You can also contact SCORE's Washington, D.C. office at 202—205–6762.

SCORE has been helping small businesses for over 25 years and should be able to find someone who has successfully solved the problems you face.

Schools offer free marketing help

Local colleges are another potential source of free marketing help. Schools, for example, are always trying to place students at local businesses so they can get real world experience. You can employ them as your needs dictate. The pay can be entry level. Best of all, you can receive low–cost but knowledgeable and eager assistance for the various marketing jobs you are too busy to tackle.

You might also ask marketing teachers to use your marketing tasks as class projects. This way, you get help from the teacher and scores of bright, eager students. Ideal class projects include market research needs, surveys, compiling mailing lists and other important but short–term activities. Don't forget other departments for help with nonmarketing needs.

SBA has free business information

The U.S. Small Business Administration exists solely to help you get into and stay in business. To assist you, SBA provides tons of free or low–cost management guides and booklets.

They have how–to brochures for just about every business. SBA also has special management, marketing, accounting and other training programs for minority entrepreneurs. Your best bet is to visit your local SBA office for details.

Take advantage of free sales aids

Check suppliers and trade groups for free sales aids before you buy your own. Many furnish point–of–purchase displays, counter cards, window items, take–one boxes, banners, posters and stickers. Some also provide information brochures, shells and other sales aids.

Shells are sheets of paper preprinted with colorful pictures, designs and other eye–grabbing gimmicks. They also have space for you to print in your own information. As a result, you can prepare colorful and illustrated sales material for the cost of black and white printing. Check with your suppliers and vendors for these items.

But don't stop there. Ask your rep for the name of the regional or divisional promotions manager. You'll find most of these people are eager to help clients and customers who are willing to do a little extra to boost sales.

Sometimes they come up with special sales tools, displays and other goodies that even your local sales rep may not know about. They may also have discretionary advertising money intended for special projects—like yours.

Small Business Development Centers

The Small Business Administration and state agencies have set up Small Business Development Centers (SBDC) in many cities. SBDCs provide free managerial and technical help, low–cost educational programs, how–to brochures and other resources for those trying to start or expand a business. Check your phone book for the nearest local SBDC.

Local government programs await you

Job creation and business development are high on the agenda of most cities today. So drop by local government offices when you begin your search for help. You'll find that many cities and counties have economic development departments that assist small businesses. They may also provide small business loans and grants in an effort to retain or attract small businesses. Local business development corporations are another resource to investigate.

Check chambers and trade groups

There are scores of other places where you can receive free marketing and general management assistance. Many of these sources also provide valuable background and research data—free—to help you make sound business decisions. For instance, local chambers of commerce frequently sponsor small business resource centers.

If you want help related to your specific field or business, contact trade and merchant associations. To get trade association names, thumb through the trade association directories available at many local libraries.

Utilities, banks another resource

Telephone, electric, gas and other public utility companies often maintain small business assistance programs. In the Midwest, for example, the Ameritech telephone company offers various free booklets for small businesses and people who work at home. Topics typically cover telephone sales, equipment and other aspects of setting up and managing a small business.. Availability changes constantly so check for the latest offerings. Your local phone company may have a similar program.

Speaking of the phone company, check the front of your Business to Business Directory—some contain a comprehensive and highly useful list of business resources.

In the past, banks often shied away from small businesses. But no longer. More and more banks now offer small business assistance programs in addition to special banking products tailored to your needs. Assistance varies from providing basic how–to booklets to full–time small business specialists. These specialists may hold workshops or help entrepreneurs prepare viable business plans.

Index

Q

R

S